S0-BXX-763

CHILD ABUSE

AN

AMERICAN

EPIDEMIC

REVISED EDITION

CHILD ABUSE

AN AMERICAN EPIDEMIC

ELAINE LANDAU

Julian Messner

Copyright © 1984, 1990 by Elaine Landau
All rights reserved including the right of
reproduction in whole or in part in any form.
Published by Julian Messner, a division of
Silver Burdett Press, Inc., Simon & Schuster, Inc.
Prentice Hall Bldg., Englewood Cliffs, NJ 07632.

JULIAN MESSNER and colophon are trademarks of
Simon & Schuster, Inc.
Design by Elaine Groh
Manufactured in the United States of America.

Lib. ed. 10 9 8 7 6 5 4 3 2 1

Paper ed. 10 9 8 7 6 5 4 3 2 1

Library of Congress Cataloging-in-Publication Data
Landau, Elaine.
Child abuse: an American epidemic / Elaine Landau.—Rev. ed.
      p.   cm.
Includes bibliographical references.
Summary: Discusses the problem of child abuse, its causes and what can
be done to prevent it. Includes a list of agencies and organizations that
provide information and help to abused children and runaways.
1. Child abuse—United States—Juvenile literature. 2. Child molesting—
United States—Juvenile literature. [1. Child abuse.]
I. Title.
HV6626.5.L36   1989   89-12772
362.7′6′0973—dc20   CIP
                            AC
ISBN 0-671-68874-X (lib bdg.)   ISBN 0-671-68875-8
(pbk.)

OTHER BOOKS BY
ELAINE LANDAU

Different Drummer
Homosexuality in America

Growing Old in America

The Homeless

On the Streets
The Lives of Adolescent Prostitutes

Teenagers Talk About School

Why Are They Starving Themselves?
Understanding Anorexia Nervosa and Bulimia

FOR LISA STEINBERG
1981 – 1987

CONTENTS

NOTE FROM
THE AUTHOR

THIS is a book about child abuse as it exists today in the American family. It deals with how and why abusive situations arise, the different forms of abuse, and how our society has often failed young abuse victims. It's a book about families in trouble and what some people are trying to do to bring changes.

CHILD ABUSE

AN
AMERICAN
EPIDEMIC

CHAPTER 1

AMERICAN TRAGEDIES

ON Kevin's third birthday, his grandmother took him out to celebrate. The two went to lunch at a Dallas coffee shop for a special birthday meal. It was a pleasant, happy time for the little boy, whose arms and legs were visibly discolored with bruises. He even had ice cream for dessert. As he ate it, the waitress was horrified to see blood leaking from the toddler's mouth.

Unfortunately, little Kevin (not his real name) was not a stranger to pain. Often he had received emergency treatment at the hospital for various cuts, bruises, and wounds. During his examinations there, physicians had detected a number of old bone fractures.

Always, Kevin's parents insisted that their son's many injuries were caused by accidents. They assured the hospital staff that the small boy was clumsy and accident prone. Although they'd tried to protect him, they said, Kevin continually hurt himself.

However, Kevin's grandmother knew differently. She was aware that the toddler had been systematically and repeatedly abused by his father. In an effort to assist her brutalized grandson, she reported these incidents to the local child-protection authorities. Her accusations were supported by the findings of the medical staff who treated Kevin and were convinced that his injuries were not accidental.

The case was investigated, but immediate help was not forthcoming for Kevin. The child's life and future were put on hold as he became little more than a number on a file. Despite numerous complaints from various individuals who had come in contact with the youngster, Kevin was never removed from his home.

Kevin's grandmother had done her best to brighten the little boy's life with the special birthday luncheon. After the meal she took her grandson back to his home. But as it turned out, Kevin didn't have the happy birthday his grandmother had wished for him.

Although the details of exactly what happened that night are still not clear, it is known that at some time during that evening Kevin's father took his son into the bedroom. His father, who was unemployed, had become angry at the child. Kevin's mother later reported that she heard a loud thumping noise coming from inside the room. Kevin didn't live through the night. His father had kicked him to death.

Child abuse that results in death is unfortunately not as uncommon as most people would like to believe. Another victim was Lisa Steinberg, a six-year-old illegally adopted girl, who'd lived in a five-story townhouse that had once been the home of Mark Twain. At 6:30 A.M. on Monday, November 2, 1987, Lisa's "adoptive" mother, Hedda Nussbaum, called 911, New York City's emergency switchboard. The panic-stricken woman requested assistance for the young girl, whom she described as having choked on an early-morning snack of vegetables.

Minutes later, the police arrived at the apartment building just off Fifth Avenue. Lisa had lived in the dark, squalid apartment with Joel Steinberg, his girlfriend, Hedda Nussbaum, and a sixteen-month-old baby boy. Like Lisa, the little boy had been illegally adopted by the couple.

The apartment's walls and floors were bare, and there was a strong odor of stale and rotted food in the air. The tiny boy sat on the floor in a urine-soaked diaper; he was tied to a playpen by a three-foot cord. Even though the apartment's electricity hadn't been turned off, none of the lights worked. The family of four had only one bed and its sheets and pillow cases were blood stained.

Officer Vincent DaLuise was the first to find

Lisa. The small girl wasn't breathing, but she still had a pulse. As the officer bent over Lisa, trying to revive her, he could clearly see that her body was covered with bruises.

An ambulance was called, and Lisa was taken to St. Vincent's Hospital. The doctors tried their best to save her, but it was too late. Lisa was already clinically dead. She'd suffered a brain hemorrhage caused by repeated blows to the head. Only the mechanical respirator next to her bed kept her breathing.

Lisa Steinberg never regained consciousness. The hospital nurses called the little girl "Sleeping Beauty" and remained at her side for three days. Then the life-support systems were disconnected and Lisa was officially declared dead. Her "adoptive" father was charged with murder.

On the surface, it looked as though Lisa Steinberg had an ideal home. Joel Steinberg was a criminal defense attorney and Hedda Nussbaum wrote and edited children's books. On outings to the neighborhood park, Steinberg had told neighbors how much he loved children.

However, by the late 1970s it became clear that the Steinberg household was one of violence. Over the years, neighbors had repeatedly called the police to report the chilling screams and loud noises that came from the apartment. Some said it sounded as though bodies were falling and remarked that at times the screaming would go on all night. Yet, though the police frequently came to the Steinberg residence, Hedda Nussbaum always refused to say that Steinberg had hit her.

After a time, Hedda lost her job at a major New York publishing house and her family situation worsened. Over the next few years, Steinberg repeatedly abused her. At home all day under Steinberg's domination, Hedda Nussbaum became reclusive and avoided friends and visitors who'd be aware of her increasingly battered appearance. Steinberg also did his best to isolate Hedda from the outside world. Once when her mother came to visit, Steinberg told the woman to leave and never come back. Steinberg also said that Hedda's sister Judith was an "evil" person whom he described as being "dangerous to us". He even forbade Hedda to speak to her family on the telephone unless he was present.

Drugs may have been a factor in the deterioration of the Steinberg-Nussbaum household. After Lisa's death, an official search of the apartment revealed stashes of marijuana, hashish, heroin, and cocaine. Digital scales to measure narcotics and crack pipes were also found in the apartment.

Neighbors attested that the rampages in the

apartment occurred regularly. But most people thought of Hedda Nussbaum as Steinberg's victim. Few believed that the outgoing and friendly little girl living with the couple had become a target for her "adoptive" father's anger and beatings.

Still, not everyone was fooled. During 1983 and 1984 two complaints of possible child abuse at the Steinberg residence were registered with New York City's Bureau of Child Welfare. However, investigators from the division determined that the allegations were unfounded and the case was dropped.

Nevertheless, there had been signs that Lisa Steinberg was in trouble at home. Shortly before her death she seemed especially sad, and on a few occasions she cried when it was time to go home at the end of the school day.

Although Lisa was an intelligent girl who was eager to learn, lately she'd seemed listless and distracted. Lisa looked unkempt. Her hair was matted and clumps of it had been cut off. She was sloppily dressed. Lisa Steinberg just did not give the appearance of a loved and well cared-for child.

Ironically, in the month before her death, Lisa Steinberg was nearly rescued twice. On October 6 police were summoned to the Steinbergs' home in response to a call from a neighbor who said that someone was being beaten inside the apartment.

At first Joel Steinberg tried to prevent the officers from entering. He told them that he was an attorney and knew his rights.

However, the police persisted and eventually gained entry to the apartment. They demanded to see Hedda Nussbaum. Hedda appeared with a freshly swollen lip, but once again she refused to file a complaint against Joel Steinberg. The police left a pamphlet for her that listed shelter sites for battered women, but she and the two children remained in the apartment.

Then, only ten days before Lisa's death, a toll taker on the New York State Thruway saw a small girl in a car that stopped at her booth. Observing that the child was bruised and sobbing, she alerted the police.

Farther down the road the highway police stopped Joel Steinberg. He explained that he was a New York lawyer returning home with his daughter after trying a case upstate. He convinced the officers that everything was all right. He told them that Lisa had been crying because she had a stiff neck. Steinberg was allowed to go on his way, and Lisa went home with him.

About a week after Lisa died, her biological mother came forward. The young woman's dealings with Steinberg had begun and ended six years before, when she'd hired him to act as her attorney in finding an adoptive home for her baby. She'd never dreamed that Steinberg intended to keep the baby for himself. Lisa's natural mother went to court to win the right to bury her daughter. She didn't want the little girl to be buried by the people who killed her. The judge granted her request.

Hedda Nussbaum was hospitalized for observation and treatment at a psychiatric center. After being taken into custody, Joel Steinberg was held for trial without bail. He pleaded not guilty to second-degree murder. The Steinberg trial proved to be one of the most gruesome child-abuse trials of the decade.

In 1989, Joel Steinberg was convicted of first-degree manslaughter in the beating death of young Lisa. He was sentenced to a maximum of eight-and-one-half to twenty-five years in prison. Manhattan Supreme Court Justice Harold Rothwax, who sentenced Steinberg, stated that "The court strongly and emphatically recommends against release of this defendant on parole." Steinberg was also fined $5,100.[1]

Unfortunately, Lisa Steinberg's fate is not unique. In New York City, a child dies of abuse and neglect every two-and-a-half days.[2]

In many such incidents, parents attempt to hide the truth of the child's death. When police found Lisa Steinberg comatose on the bathroom floor, Hedda Nussbaum said that the child had choked on vegetables. Later Joel Steinberg described the young girl's many injuries as the result of having "fallen a lot" on roller skates.

The list of "accidents" common to abuse victims is lengthy. Young people are said to have drowned or been scalded by hot water while bathing, suffocated under their own pillows while sleeping, and fallen from chairs, couches, tables, bicycles, and windows.

Often the children die. It has been estimated that as of the late 1980s, approximately thirteen hundred children in the United States die each year from child abuse.[3] Sixty-five percent of them are toddlers, less than two years of age. These statistics represent only the cases on record. It's generally believed that thousands of cases go unreported each year and that many more deaths from beatings are disguised as accidents.

The children who survive continue to live a life of horror. Some may have been permanently crippled or maimed; others have suffered brain damage as the result of the very severe punishments inflicted on them. All are victims of abuse and neglect.

A great deal of abuse goes on in secret in the privacy of people's homes. Often the abusive parents do not take the child for medical treatment unless they think the child's life might be in serious danger, at which point they become frightened by the possible ramifications of having, perhaps unwittingly, committed a murder. When the child is taken to a doctor, the parents claim that they can't imagine how the child could have been injured or they offer an unlikely explanation of what happened.

In order to disguise revealing scars or symptoms that might point to child abuse, many abusive parents try not to return to the same doctor or hospital. If these parents are asked about their child's general health or history of accidents, their descriptions do not always support even the most obvious conclusions drawn from X-rays and examinations.

In many cases X-rays have revealed broken bones in different stages of healing, indicating that the injuries to the child were inflicted on separate occasions. The manner in which the bone repairs itself can also provide physicians with important information about the nature of the injury. Even if the parents claim that the child's arm was broken by a fall, X-rays may reveal that the bone actually snapped from being roughly twisted or pulled.

Too often we only hear about the most

"sensationalized" cases of abuse: those that reach television, radio, and newspapers. Stories of babies left to die in garbage cans, incinerators, and subway stations have regrettably become all too common. However, more subtle forms of abuse take place in households across the country on a daily basis. The signs of abuse and neglect need not be a small body covered with scars or a child who has had both legs broken in numerous places. An abused young person may be a child who behaves like a frightened, wounded animal shuddering at the friendly touch of another human being.

An abused child may be one who is severely dehydrated or on the verge of starvation. Maltreatment and neglect may also be evinced by a child with infected sores that have not been attended to, or even by a youngster who continually suffers from a bad case of lice.

Many children are severely neglected by those responsible for their care. Instances of blatant neglect may be less shocking and dramatic than those of abuse, but the effects of prolonged neglect can be just as devastating to the young person's well-being.

There are many ways of neglecting a child. A parent may fail to give him adequate food, a sanitary home environment, or sufficient and appropriate clothing. In some instances the adult may show disregard or disdain for the child's educational, medical, or emotional needs. Neglected children are often denied the love, supervision, and emotional support that are crucial to a normal and healthy transition into adulthood.

Among the deadliest forms of child neglect are cases of inadequate supervision. According to Robert Sabreen, regional administrator of the New Jersey Division of Youth and Family Services (DYFS), "The younger the child, the longer the child is left alone, the greater the chances that the lack of supervision may lead to a fatality."

Every year young children die when their parents go out and leave them alone. At times, these children have even fallen out of windows. As Mr. Sabreen said, "You can have a fire—that is very common, particularly in urban areas. The parent goes out, nobody knows that there's a child inside, and the child is too young to get out."[4]

A baby has no ability to care for himself. Usually his parents look out for his welfare, speak up for his rights, and safeguard him from harm. But at times some element within the framework goes amiss and the child's well-being is threatened by the very people who are responsible for his protection.

HOW AND WHY IT HAPPENS

A seven-year-old boy had been admitted to intensive-care units over a dozen times since the age of two. The child had suffered various internal injuries from his father's punches and kicks to his stomach. One time the boy's enraged mother slashed his cheek with a butcher knife and cut off a portion of his left ear. The same child had so often been beaten in the face with an iron skillet that there was nothing left of his nose.

How can child abuse in America continue after so many cases of violence against young people have been documented? Any examination of child abuse requires questioning a basic assumption of our society: "The parent owns the child."

Perhaps this premise was first challenged in 1874, when the earliest child-abuse case in America was brought to court. It all started when one day Henry Bergh, founder of the ASPCA, was combing the streets of New York City in search of wounded and abused animals. As Bergh walked past an apartment building, he heard a child's screams from inside.

Bergh ran into the apartment to find a ten-year-old girl named Mary Ellen being repeatedly stabbed with a pair of scissors by her parents. Mary Ellen's mother and father thought that their young daughter was a witch.

Henry Bergh wanted to take the child away from her parents, but at the time there weren't any child-abuse laws in existence. He argued in court for Mary Ellen's safety on the ground that children should be entitled to protection from abuse just as dogs and cats were.

Formerly it was assumed that children didn't need protection from their own parents. Mothers and fathers supposedly acted only in the best interests of their children. Discipline and supervision were left solely in the parents' hands. It was as if children belonged to their parents and in many ways were considered their property.

Unfortunately, remnants of this assumption still exist. Parental discipline is supposedly administered for the child's own good, but in many instances child abuse has been committed in the name of discipline. Children are generally not thought to need protection because they have parents to look out for them, although many times children do need protection—from their own parents.

As Donald Bross, a lawyer, medical sociologist, and advocate for abused children stated, "We still think of children as their parents' private property—

and that is the heart of the problem. Yes, family privacy is a good thing, but not in the case of the battered wife or the abused child."[1]

At times it is difficult to know when outside intervention is appropriate. In at least one community, people were so outraged by the removal of children from an abusive, neglectful home that bomb threats were made against the social services building.[2]

Some citizens strongly feel that government shouldn't meddle in people's lives or that judges, attorneys, and social workers have no right to tell people how to bring up their own children. It is not uncommon for social workers to hear of well-intentioned people who suspected trouble at a neighbor's house, but were reluctant to become involved because they felt it didn't concern them. Until those priorities are changed, more and more children will die.

Parents do not own their children. They merely care for them in trust for the rest of society. To maximize healthy growth and development, all children should grow up surrounded by social relationships that are close, personal, and enduring.

When a newborn infant leaves the hospital with his parents, the child's progress may not come to the attention of any social institution until he enters school at the age of four or five. If his parents are responsible, mature individuals who are capable of adequately meeting his needs for nurture and protection, all will go well for him. However, abuse may arise when parental power is misused.

Parental authority and power are misused when they are employed to damage the child either physically or emotionally, or administered in any manner that reduces or limits the child's opportunity for normal growth and development. The absolute authority of the parent is rarely questioned in our society when it is exercised judiciously with no visible harmful effects. The important ethical question of whether the child has a right to his own integrity as a separate individual is generally left unexamined.

What common factors are present in homes with abusive parent-child relationships? Social isolation seems to be a major component. Ours is a highly mobile society. Job changes and educational needs frequently take people to new parts of the country. Often they live far from their relatives and don't develop strong new ties to a church or synagogue. In many instances, it's hard to initiate new friendships with busy neighbors who have tight schedules.

This may leave the parent at home with a baby or small child in a stressful predicament. Being cut off from support systems that might enable the parent to deal more effectively with the frustrations inherent in caring for a small child can lead to abuse.

Kate, an attractive redhead in her early thirties, left her job at a bank when her son was born. She planned to devote all of her time to the baby. But unfortunately, it wasn't long before she began to regret her decision. Her husband, a successful administrator, was away at work for about ten hours a day, while Kate was left by herself with the baby in their eastern Massachusetts home.

Their son was a colicky infant who had trouble sleeping and seemed to cry most of the time. Kate found herself unprepared for the loneliness and exhaustion she experienced as a new parent. She missed her old friends from work. Her family was hundreds of miles away, and she didn't know any mothers with very young children.

Kate became depressed. She began to hold her infant son responsible for her unhappiness. Kate felt that she hated the baby for what her life had become.

Before long Kate found herself hitting her son at the slightest provocation. The infant had merely to drop his bottle to feel the sting of her hand. To hide any bruises, Kate made certain that her blows landed only on the baby's back. She took care never to hit his face.

Kate knew that what she was doing was wrong, but she couldn't seem to stop herself. Afterward, she always felt remorseful. She said, "Every time I hit him, I would cry and apologize and promise him that Mommy would never do it again."

At that point Kate thought that she had to be the world's worst mother. She felt she was probably the only person in suburbia who hit her own baby.

But she was wrong. Child abuse in America has reached epidemic proportions. Over 2.2 million cases of child abuse and neglect are reported every year.[3]

Disciplinary situations are more likely to turn into child abuse in families that are socially isolated or cut off from support networks that could intervene and provide help. A parent in a stressful situation is far less likely to be abusive to his child if he can turn to another person or a social agency for assistance. Often just being able to ask a relative or friend to take the child out for a few hours or for a weekend can make a difference.

Support can also be provided by play groups, such as those sponsored by a church or social agency. While the children are there, the parents can relax and have a chance to let off some steam or gather their thoughts. They may simply need a break from an exasperating situation.

Support systems generally arise through a sense of connectedness with the community. A parent or family in trouble needs a variety of resources to call upon in times of personal crisis or excessive stress. Such resource people might include the extended family, other parents, clergy, educators, social workers, mental health practitioners, and others.

Unfortunately, abusive parents may tend to distrust and retreat from society. Parents who habitually abuse their children generally prefer not to seek help in resolving crises. In addition, abusive parents often attempt to prevent their children from forming normal healthy relationships outside the home.

Deborah Daro, research director of the National Committee for the Prevention of Child Abuse, said of the Steinberg case, "Though Lisa Steinberg was an exception to the rule in many ways, in other ways her family was typical of the child-abuse home. The family was isolated from other families and friends. . . ."[4]

Of course, everyone needs some privacy, and lack of social contact does not *cause* abuse or neglect. No one factor produces the same reaction in all people. Depending on their individual circumstances, some children may find themselves more vulnerable than others. Still, isolation has been identified as a known factor that places the parent-child relationship in special jeopardy. In America, privacy and an individual's right to it have become a treasured ideal. However, each year hundreds of thousands of children pay for their parents' privacy with their tears.

Substance abuse is also a factor that may intensify stressful parent-child relationships. At least forty percent of all abuse cases involve the parent's use of alcohol or drugs. Alcohol has long been a catalyst in domestic violence, but the growing use of crack in recent years has served to worsen matters. Loretta Kowal of the Massachusetts Society for the Prevention of Cruelty to Children stated, "Crack can turn a loving mother into a monster in ten minutes."[5]

In the beating death of Lisa Steinberg, the comatose girl was left to lie naked for hours on a bathroom floor, while her "adoptive" parents free-based cocaine.[6] Darwin Carlisle's mother was on cocaine when she left her nine-year-old daughter locked alone in an apartment for nearly a week in January. The Gary, Indiana, child suffered a severe case of frostbite. Both her legs had to be amputated at the knee. Darwin's twenty-five-year-old mother pleaded guilty to felony child neglect and was sentenced to fourteen years in prison.[7]

The National Committee for the Prevention of Child Abuse estimates that in as many as forty percent of the deaths due to child abuse, the abusive parent had a drug or alcohol problem. Substance abuse impairs thinking and judgment, lessens inhibitions, and often acts as a barrier in preventing parents from coming to grips with problems.

A third common component in child abuse is its connection with wife beating. In thirty to forty percent of child-abuse cases, the wife was also a victim of physical abuse.[8] Since four to six million women are abused each year by their husbands and boyfriends, the number of children in jeopardy is overwhelming. Lisa Steinberg's "adoptive" mother, Hedda Nussbaum, had been abused by Joel Steinberg for over a decade at the time of Lisa's death.[9] A fourth element that may contribute to child abuse is the fact that many child-abuse victims grow up to become abusers themselves. Often adults who mistreat their children are found to have little or poor preparation for their role as parents. They have no history of good experiences as children. They lack appropriate role models on which to pattern their behavior as parents. Someone who was never given a sense of dignity and self-esteem as a young person may find it difficult to provide his own child with either a sense of well-being and worthiness or appropriate discipline.

Parents who were abused children are six times more likely to abuse their own children than are parents from "normal" homes.[10] Dr. Vincent Fontana, who in 1962 first identified the "maltreatment syndrome in children" and designed a specialized program to aid abusive parents and their children at New York Foundling Hospital, explained, "These parents never had parental love and care themselves. They don't know what being a loving parent is. Many of these people have been programmed for violence, and some of them expect their little children to 'parent' them. When the child does not provide this mothering or fathering—when the child cries or has a temper tantrum—they think this means 'I hate you,' and they strike out at the child."[11]

Parents who were themselves emotionally impoverished often experience a great deal of trouble learning the role of parent. Many lack insight and knowledge in dealing with infants and children, and they often express unrealistic expectations about their offspring.

Although significant research exists to support

the theory that abusive behavior repeats itself in successive generations, studies conducted by researchers Joan Kaufman and Edward Ziegler indicate that this need not always be the case. In certain situations, mitigating factors have altered the effects of the environment on the child.

Their studies show that abused children who as adults have a loving, supportive relationship with a spouse or lover, as well as those who are aware of having a history of abuse and are consciously resolved not to repeat it, are more likely to break the cycle. As Kaufman and Ziegler found, "Being maltreated as a child puts one at risk for becoming abusive, but the path between these two points is far from direct or inevitable."[12]

A final factor in the incidence of child abuse often proves to be a general lack of parenting skills. When a person becomes a parent he must undergo a definite series of changes. He has to reorganize his values and priorities to include a baby. He must set aside the immediate gratification of his own needs, as the helpless child must now come first. Abusive parents have often been described as individuals who experience difficulty in balancing their own needs against the needs of their child.

A person who has not learned to function as a competent parent may find a nearly intolerable situation even further aggravated by outside factors. An unwanted or unplanned pregnancy, seemingly relentless demands from older children in the family, overwork or job-related problems, financial difficulties, and countless other sources of stress may eventually help to create an abusive family situation.

Anne, a former elementary school teacher, experienced problems in parenting her two-year-old daughter. Every time Anne was about to leave the house, her daughter would have a tantrum.

Anne didn't know how to discipline her child effectively. She'd ask her to behave in a pleasant manner, but the little girl refused to listen. Meanwhile, Anne began to feel inadequate and angry. Finally, she'd reach her boiling point. Then Anne would roughly shake and push the child.

The most upsetting incident took place when Anne told her daughter to take a nap and the child refused. Anne sat on the child to hold her down while she placed a pillow over her daughter's head. The child cried and screamed, but her mother persisted.

Finally, Anne realized that her child was gasping for air. That made Anne stop, but she knew now that if she didn't get help soon, she might one day kill her daughter in anger. Both the mother and child were frightened.

Anne was fortunate that she was able to secure effective help immediately. She contacted a local chapter of the National Exchange Club, an organization that offers counseling in such situations. Anne began to learn new parenting skills that helped her to deal with her daughter in a more positive way.

Anne realized that she'd been trying to be a perfect mother, and that such unrealistic expectations only added to the frustrations of child rearing. She learned that it's better to "blow off steam" occasionally than to let the pressure build up inside to a dangerous boiling point. Now when tensions arise between Anne and her daughter, she sends the little girl to her room until they've both had an opportunity to regain their composure.

Although many people believe that poverty increases the likelihood of child abuse, no one knows for certain. The National Committee for the Prevention of Child Abuse has reported numerous instances of abuse by people from well-to-do, well-educated families. In addition, Dr. Eli Newburger, director of the Family Development Study at Children's Hospital in Boston, has stressed that violence in middle- and upper-class homes is far more common than is generally known. Middle-class professional parents may know how to look for help discreetly. These parents may also have a more sophisticated understanding of how to shift suspicion from themselves when talking to teachers, doctors, and police.

According to a nationwide survey of hospitals conducted by Newburger, it was race and social status of the family, not the severity of the child's injuries, that determined whether doctors reported suspected abuse cases to the authorities as they are required to do by law. Newburger believes that too often physicians have a stereotyped view of a child abuser and tend not to suspect a parent who doesn't conform to that negative image.

Another dangerous tendency cited by Dr. Newburger is that physicians may deliberately look the other way when faced with child abuse involving their more affluent patients. Many middle-class families use a physician whom they've known and trusted for years. These doctors may feel hesitant to report their patients to the authorities and betray their confidence. They also may be reluctant to lose steady clients. At times physicians' desire to maintain a good doctor-patient relationship with their clients has been placed above the overall welfare of a child.[13]

In many cases of middle-class child abuse, psychiatrists may prefer to sedate the abuser rather than tackle the real underlying problem. Sandy, a young mother who lived in a rambling New England home with her husband and their seven-month-old son, sought the help of a therapist when she realized that she couldn't stop abusing her baby. However, instead of giving Sandy a chance to discuss her problems and feelings with him, the psychiatrist handed her a prescription for a tranquilizer.

Unfortunately, Sandy's experience is not unusual. Dr. Richard D. Krugman, director of the C. Henry Kempe National Center for the Prevention and Treatment of Child Abuse and Neglect in Denver, has said that what happened to Sandy happens all too often, though people are hesitant to believe it. Dr. Krugman, who feels this kind of treatment is a stain on the psychiatric profession, stresses that in such instances the doctor never gets to the root of the parent's anger. As a result, the child is left at risk.[14]

The Parents Anonymous Hotline, which confidentially helps parents who have been, or fear becoming, violent with their children, reports that many of its calls come from middle-class people. But child-abuse cases among the middle class still tend to shock the public. It is always difficult to believe that things could go so wrong for people like Joel Steinberg and Hedda Nussbaum, who seemingly have so much. Middle-class child abuse defies the American dream and tarnishes the myth of the "ideal family." Child abuse is always supposed to happen "somewhere else." But in reality it can happen anywhere.

CHAPTER 3

EMOTIONAL ABUSE

ONE afternoon seven-year-old Russell Baptist sat tied to a chair on the front lawn of a housing complex in Hayward, California. Tied over his nose was a cardboard pig snout made from an egg carton. Pinned to the small boy's shirt was a sign fashioned by his mother, which read, "I'm a dumb pig. Ugly is what you become every time you lie and steal. My hands are tied because I cannot be trusted. This is a lesson to be learned. Look. Laugh. Thief. Stealing. Bad Boy." A cluster of neighbors had gathered around Russell to read the cruelty scribbled on this small human billboard. Because Russell's hands were tightly bound, he was unable to wipe away the tears that streamed down his cheeks.

Russell's mother, twenty-nine-year-old Mary Bergamasco, who as a result of her actions faced losing custody of her son, had not had an easy childhood herself. The punishment she devised for Russell was similar to the way she had been punished when she had stolen as a child. Ms. Bergamasco claimed that her mother also burned her hands to teach her a lesson.

Russell's case was heard in Alameda County

Superior Court. Ms. Bergamasco told the court that she had only resorted to the pig punishment after other attempts at disciplining her son had failed. According to his mother, Russell had stolen some baseball cards, a belt buckle, six dollars, and another child's toy. In her defense, Mary Bergamasco's attorney, Melvin Belli, described his client as a "good mother who loves her children." He added, "God knows we all make mistakes."[1]

In court, Russell testified that he still loves his mother, but that he'd rather live with his father. The young boy said that his father never embarrassed him and would teach him to water ski.

Anne Cohn, executive director for the National Committee for the Prevention of Child Abuse, feels that Mary Bergamasco is guilty of emotionally abusing her son. Ms. Cohn believes that Ms. Bergamasco's choice of punishment was humiliating, embarrassing, and degrading to Russell. She feels that emotional abuse may be the most heinous form of child abuse. Ms. Cohn points out that while broken bones heal fairly quickly, broken spirits mend much less easily.[2]

In recent years, numerous child-development researchers have focused their work on the effects of emotional child abuse. Their findings support the idea that abuse of this nature can be as devastating as brutal physical punishment—sometimes even more devastating.[3]

Although the National Committee for the Prevention of Child Abuse receives approximately 250,000 reports of emotional child abuse each year, its employees believe that the actual incidence may be significantly higher.[4] Like physical abuse, emotional abuse cuts across racial, ethnic, and income lines. It can happen in any home where parents reject, humiliate, or resort to harsh and degrading forms of punishment.

In some ways the dynamics behind emotional abuse are similar to those of physical abuse. A destructive pattern of emotional abuse may be passed from one generation to the next. James Garbarino, president of the Erikson Institute for the Advanced Study of Child Development, contends that a parent will tend to repeat what he's familiar with unless he learns more effective ways of disciplining his child.[5] In addition, parents who are forced to deal with the stresses of unemployment, alcohol or drug abuse, and social isolation may be more likely than others to lash out emotionally at their children.

Emotional child abuse may not be challenged as frequently as physical abuse because it's less tangible and more difficult to define and pinpoint. But that doesn't make it any less real.

One common form of emotional child abuse is verbal assault. Verbal assault or abuse humiliates or degrades the young person. When a parent verbally abuses a child, he uses words in a punitive and destructive manner. Verbal abuse damages the child's self-esteem and undermines his confidence. It's difficult to develop and maintain a sense of personal pride or dignity when you're continually told by people who matter to you that you are little more than worthless garbage.

An especially cruel instance of verbal abuse against a child took place in a bar when a father decided to demonstrate his power over his preschool daughter by showing his friends how easily he could make her cry. The man beckoned the little girl over to the bar stools, where he proceeded to call her a series of obscene and humiliating names.

He forced her to stand there and agree with everything he said. The girl did as she was told, but tears spilled down her cheeks as her father continued. At that point the girl's father started to laugh, indicating to the others how easily he could make the child cry without even touching her.[6]

Young children have no way to handle that kind of overwhelming public humiliation from parents, the people who should shield them from embarrassment and hurt. Children believe what their parents tell them. If children hear only that they are stupid, lazy, and good for nothing, before long they believe that's exactly what they are.

Pediatric therapists stress that even in moments of extreme anger, it is important for parents not to label their children with such words as "jerk," "stupid," "dumb," or "good for nothing." Although children need to know that parents have set limits, discipline must be carried out within a context of love and respect. Positive discipline should not be tinged with hostility. Parents can be strict without crushing the child's spirit.[7]

Four-year-old Teddy had been a disappointment to his parents from the time he was born. Teddy's parents, both professionals, regretted that their son hadn't inherited his mother's good looks and that he showed almost no interest in the new computer they had purchased for him.

Teddy's parents continually criticized their son. They made the child feel guilty for acting like the four-year-old he was. His mother complained that he failed to appreciate all that she and her husband did for him. She told Teddy he was too messy. She was also annoyed at the little boy for spending so much time just looking at her with his large, sad eyes.

Teddy's mother often dealt angrily and abusively

with her child. Although the boy's table manners were typical of a four-year-old's, his mother accused him of deliberately being untidy. When Teddy accidentally dribbled his milk while eating cereal, his mother was sure that he did it purposely to aggravate her. As punishment, she placed her son's cereal bowl on the floor. Then she told Teddy to eat from the floor as an animal would because that's all he really was.[8]

Parents who emotionally abuse their children generally tend to ignore positive, healthy behavior exhibited by the child and instead concentrate on the child's faults. Often they emphasize even the child's minor unpleasant or incorrect actions.

Gary was another four-year-old victim of emotional child abuse. His stepfather, a sheriff's deputy, was determined to make the preschooler behave in a manly fashion. The man often deliberately placed the child in frightening situations and then taunted and ridiculed him if he appeared frightened or broke down in tears.

Once his stepfather described to Gary a certain closet in the house, which he said was filled with vampire bats. He told the boy that first the bats suck out your blood and then they kill you. When he felt certain that the young boy was terrified, he threw Gary into the closet, locked the door, and walked away.

The four-year-old began to scream for his life. Gary cried so hard and long that after a few hours his voice became hoarse. When he was finally let out of the closet, the child was bloody as a result of broken blood vessels in his throat from his intense crying. Gary's mother took him to a doctor for his injuries, but she staunchly defended her husband's treatment of her child. She claimed that he was just trying to make a man of the little boy.[9]

Although some parents may resort to emotional abuse in the hope of changing their child's behavior, experts generally agree that belittlement, denigration, and other forms of verbal assault on children are cruel and ineffective ways to teach proper behavior. Children do not do better in response to being made to feel worse.

Another form of emotional abuse is psychological neglect. A parent who psychologically neglects his child is someone who either refuses or is unable to provide the child with the emotional warmth and compassion necessary for positive growth and development. The parent who psychologically neglects his child is actually emotionally absent when it comes to showing kindness or caring.

In many ways, the important nurturing bonds between parent and child are never fully developed. The child may not be severely physically punished and his basic daily physical needs may be met, but very little else is done for him.

Kevin, a year-and-a-half-old boy, is a prime example of a psychologically neglected child. Kevin's mother, an unwed teenager, did only what was minimally required to care for her son. She fed him and changed his diapers, but often she did so only after Kevin had sat for hours in a urine-soaked diaper.

Having herself been deprived of a childhood filled with love and caring, Kevin's mother found it difficult to give much to her own baby. She did not cradle or play with Kevin. She never rocked him, sang to him, or told him stories.

Kevin's mother avoided looking into his eyes and rarely smiled at her child. The contact between mother and son was kept to a minimum. Although Kevin wasn't physically abused, he was never made to feel loved.[10]

Psychologically neglected children come from homes in which they are given very little emotional security and support. Their home environment lacks warmth, and as a result they never feel a sense of being loved and wanted.

Another form of emotional abuse is exploitation of the child by the parent for the parent's own gratification. In such situations, the parent may try to make the child feel that his only purpose should be to help and please his parents.

If the child wishes to follow his own dreams or pursue activities of his own choosing, the parent may try to make the young person feel guilty, ungrateful, and worthless. These children are never made to feel loved for being themselves; their worthiness is dependent on their obedience and their ability to please. Parents who exploit their children in this way do not see their offspring as separate individuals but as little more than extensions of themselves.

Becky was a thirteen-year-old who, despite her youth, was largely responsible for caring for her ill mother as well as for most of the general upkeep of the family's residence. From the time she was ten, Becky was required to do much of the housekeeping and all of the cooking for her family. Every day after school she'd hurry home to care for her younger brother and begin a long list of household duties. Becky's role as the family's "housekeeper" continued even after her mother's degenerative nerve disease went into remission and the woman felt much better.

One day, after Becky had completed her home-work and duties around the house, she asked her mother's permission to spend some time with the friends she'd made at school. But her mother was outraged that Becky wanted to spend her free time away from home. She called her daughter selfish, ungrateful, and irresponsible, and accused her of not caring about her own mother. She went on and on, reminding the girl of even the slightest ways in which she felt Becky could have been more thoughtful.

After that, whenever Becky expressed a desire to be with her friends, her mother always reacted in much the same way. After a while Becky came to think of herself as being a bad person for wanting a life of her own after her mother had been so sick. She thought that perhaps she had failed her mother and that maybe she ought not to mention the things she'd like for herself.

It's unfortunate that Becky's mother did not real-ize how selfish she had been in demanding that Becky put aside everything the girl liked to do. Her need to control her daughter resulted in tactics that served to lower Becky's self-esteem.

Becky wasn't allowed to be a child—instead it had become her responsibility to parent her mother. Becky's mother expected her daughter to comfort her regardless of the cost to Becky's own social growth and development. Becky was expected to suppress her own needs in favor of her mother's.[11]

Emotional abuse may be a less concrete concept than physical abuse, but its effects are clearly visible in the emotionally abused child's behavior. Name calling and cruel remarks, threats, reminders of past offenses to humiliate the young person, and attempts to instill guilt in the child are all facets of emotional abuse. Parents who behave this way produce a child who feels worthless and inadequate. At times, these children may develop a devastating feeling of hopelessness. In some instances, where there was no intervention, these children have even taken their own lives.[12]

Children from emotionally abusive homes may develop various ways of coping in order to survive. For example, they are often unusually wary of the adults around them. They may pay a great deal of attention to the mood changes and the facial expressions and body language of the grown-ups in charge of their lives.

By attempting to remain in tune with their parents, they hope to avoid angering or annoying them, and thereby to avoid subsequent humiliation and punishment. Numerous psychotherapists have noted the changeable nature of emotionally abused children's personalities and the way their behavior shifts with the needs of the moment.[13]

Another consequence of emotional abuse is that these children may tend to inhibit or limit their own goals and activities. They do this to avoid being ridiculed. If a child's words and deeds have made him the object of humiliation, he may find it safer to simply keep quiet and do as little as possible.

Rather than do something "wrong," such young people tend to be more comfortable "playing dumb." It is not uncommon for their teachers to be amazed by how high these children score on achievement tests, because they have been so careful to hide their abilities in class.[14]

However, not all emotionally abused children react to their environment in the same manner. There are other negative consequences of emotional abuse. Dr. Alayne Yates, a psychiatrist at the University of Arizona College of Medicine in Tucson, studied fifty emotionally abused children over a six-year period. Yates determined from her research that these children generally fell into three distinct categories.

The first group were the destructive children. These children demonstrated a great deal of anger and frequently destroyed property or injured people and small animals, with little sign of remorse. They appeared to have poor control over their impulses. Yates referred to the second and largest group of emotionally abused young people as the frightened children. These children appeared frightened and tried to avoid contact with people. Although they were considerably easier to get along with than the destructive children, they frequently exhibited negative behavior as well. Many of these children stole or lied compulsively. To please the adult in charge, they would agree to do nearly anything asked of them, only to turn around and do the opposite.

Yates's third group of emotionally abused children were the private children. The private children had an uncanny knack of adapting their behavior to meet the demands of others. Although these children learned to be outstanding people pleasers, they were unable to develop real attachments to others. Some did not even cling to a favorite object such as a doll or a teddy bear. Some such children appeared particularly bright and attractive to adults. However, their desire to please was usually grounded in fear of being hurt or humiliated, rather than in expectation of praise or pleasure in accomplishment.

Private children tend to adapt to difficult situations with ease. On the surface there seems to be nothing wrong with them. However, the absence of troublesome behavior doesn't erase their feelings of emptiness and anger at having spent their young lives pleasing others. Often the rage remains tightly bottled inside them for years, only to explode under stressful circumstances in adulthood.[15]

Another study was conducted by Ronald P. Kohner, Ph.D., a professor of anthropology at the University of Connecticut, and Evelyn C. Bettauer, Ph.D., a psychologist at the Sheldon Child Guidance Clinic in New Britain, Connecticut. It revealed that some rejected children tend to become clingy and possessive. It seems that if the child's needs for affection and warmth are initially unmet, he increases his efforts to win love by becoming extremely dependent.

However, this was found to be true only up to a point. If the child still isn't able to win his parents over, this response stops. As a result, many rejected children grow into adulthood unable to give love, because they never received it as young people. They don't have the necessary models on which to pattern their behavior.

Additionally, despite the fact that rejected children still crave love, after a time they don't know how to accept it. Rejected children are often unable to develop deep and satisfying relationships with others. They may tend to withdraw ever deeper into themselves.

As these children become adults, they may still feel an overwhelming need for affection. However, they are often unable to return affection after years of protecting themselves from unpleasant personal relationships. When they become parents, they may tend to reject their children as they were rejected, because that's all they know. As a result the unhealthy cycle is perpetuated.[16]

There are many different types of emotionally abusive families. Some are very poor, whereas others are exceptionally affluent. Emotionally abusive parents are found among the unemployed as well as among people in highly prestigious jobs. Emotionally abusive parents may be married or single. The one unfortunate trait these parents all share is that they either willfully or unknowingly crush and destroy their children's joy in living.

Every child is entitled to decent treatment. This means being cared for by someone who does not inflict his or her own needs on the child at the child's expense. It means having a parent who will not reject an infant's smiles, a toddler's curiosity in exploring his environment, or a school child's desire to make new friends and feel accepted by the people around him.

CHAPTER 4

SEXUAL ABUSE

CHERYL Pierson was a pretty seventeen-year-old cheerleader at Newfield High School in Selden, New York. Until her mother's death when Cheryl was sixteen, the teenager had lived in a comfortable Long Island home with her parents, her older brother, and her younger sister.

On the surface, Cheryl might seem to have had an enviable life. But this was far from the truth. Cheryl claimed that from the time she was eleven years old, her two-hundred-forty-pound father had been sexually abusing her. Mr. Pierson's abuse of his daughter had increased until he engaged in sexual intercourse with the young girl as often as three times a day. Cheryl indicated that her father had even molested her in the car on the way to see her dying mother in the hospital. As Cheryl described her predicament, "It was awful. I felt hopeless."[1]

While Cheryl's mother was hospitalized, Cheryl and her father would fall asleep watching television together in her parents' bedroom. However, after a point she realized that her father's advances toward her were wrong. Still, she allowed him to continue. There were three reasons why she acted as she did: She was afraid of her father; she didn't want to burden her mother with more pain at an already difficult time; and lastly, her father had repeatedly told her that if she dared to speak up, no one would believe her.

Cheryl thought that she'd just have to try to live through it. Whenever she refused to submit to her father's demands or started to cry, her father would take out his anger on the whole family. So to try to make everyone happy and keep peace in her home, Cheryl did her father's bidding. Besides, when Cheryl finally threatened to tell someone what was really happening, her father warned her that if she did, she'd regret it.

Cheryl had a boyfriend named Rob Cuccio who was a senior at her high school. Initially Cheryl's father had refused to allow her to go out with Rob. However, after a time he relented, permitting Cheryl to date Rob on weekends if she returned home by eleven.

However, Cheryl was fearful of being away from home for extended periods of time. She was worried about what her father would do to her younger sister while she was away. At times she would return home to find her little sister, Joann, watching television with her father under the covers or wrestling with him on the couch. Cheryl too vividly remembered that that was how her father first began sexually abusing her.

There were times when Cheryl didn't feel that she could keep what was happening to herself any longer. Sometimes, she'd pause in front of the "Time Out" lounge at her school, where students could talk with faculty advisers about problems they were unable to discuss at home. But Cheryl felt too hopeless to take any decisive action. She was embarrassed about her experiences and thought that no one would believe her.

However, what Cheryl feared most was that if she told, the school would contact her father. She often thought about the television movies she'd seen about incest. In each the father had to leave the home for a time. Yet by the end of the film, the family always reunited, and that meant that the father came home. Cheryl didn't take any action. She was too afraid of what would happen to her when her father eventually returned home. She was unable to forget her father's threat that she'd regret it if she told anyone.

Then one day Cheryl was sitting in her homeroom, discussing with her classmate Sean Pica a newspaper article about an abused wife who had enlisted someone to murder her husband. Cheryl wondered out loud who would be crazy enough to go along with a scheme like that. Sean Pica promptly indicated that he'd be willing to for the right price.

Cheryl asked him how much money would be required and Sean told her it would cost about a thousand dollars. Cheryl told her classmate that she might know someone who was interested. Several days afterward she admitted to Sean that she was that person.

Three months later, Sean shot Cheryl's father with a rifle. James Pierson, the forty-two-year-old electrician, was killed as he left home one morning for work.

A few days later, the local police received a call from an unidentified student. The caller told the authorities that Cheryl had been looking for a "hit man" to kill her father. Cheryl was brought to police headquarters for questioning, where she confessed to her part in the crime.

Before her trial, Cheryl spoke of her mixed feelings about her father. Cheryl said that she missed the part of him that was a father—the part of him that took her riding on his motorcycle and did things with her that a father is supposed to do. She claimed that was the part of him she loved.[2]

Once Cheryl's allegations of repeated sexual

abuse were made public, there were those who said that they'd suspected as much all along. A neighbor claimed that one day Cheryl's eight-year-old sister had come over to their house and openly announced that Cheryl had slept with their daddy last night. Another person saw James Pierson grab his daughter's breast while jostling with her at a 7-Eleven store. Others may have been suspicious as well, but no one ever came forward. Some weren't certain that their assumptions were on target, while others felt it was none of their business in any case.

Both Cheryl Pierson and Sean Pica pleaded guilty to manslaughter. Sean was sentenced to eight to twenty-four years in prison. Cheryl Pierson's attorney argued that the many years of sexual abuse had pushed her over the edge. The judge, who believed that Cheryl had been molested by her father, sentenced her to six months in jail and five years on probation. Cheryl is quoted as saying, while she was serving time at the Suffolk County Correctional Facility, "This is not a place I want to be in, but nothing could compare with what I went through. I just couldn't see any other way out."[3]

Incest is the least talked-about as well as the least reported form of child abuse. However, unfortunately, it is extremely prevalent in the United States.

By the late 1980s, there were over 750,000 adult women (approximately the population of the city of Baltimore) who had been victims of father-daughter incest.[4]

When a parent coerces a child into any type of sexual encounter, the protective bond between them is broken. The child is forced, through the use of his body, to pay for the normal care and affection that should be given freely. It doesn't matter whether the actual sexual contacts are brutal or pleasurable; the effect on the child's normal emotional and sexual development is always destructive.

Female children are more often subject to sexual assault than young boys. In most cases the aggressors are not strangers, but rather neighbors, family friends, uncles, stepfathers, and fathers. Sexual exploitation by a known and trusted adult has unfortunately become a reality for some young people.

Incest between mothers and sons is less common. A large number of mother-son incest incidents involve the rape of the mother by an adolescent boy. When a young boy is molested by a parent, the aggressor is as likely to be his father as his mother.

Incestuous fathers come from various socioeconomic levels. To the outside world these families may appear normal or at times even seem to be models of the all-American ideal. Many present a fairly solid front of respectability. Often the fathers have a stable employment history and the family may attend church services regularly and participate in related social functions. However, behind closed doors there usually isn't very much meaningful communication between family members. Often the parents have an unspoken agreement not to rock the boat.

In many incestuous families the traditional divisions of labor exist among family members. The men are most often regarded as the breadwinners, and the women are the homemakers. The father usually presides over the family as the unquestioned head of the household. Roles are quite distinctly defined and are usually rigidly adhered to. Often these fathers discourage their wives from engaging in activities or forming social contacts outside the home. The girls may be strongly discouraged from making friends or engaging in extracurricular activities at school.

It is not uncommon for incestuous fathers to dominate their families through the use of violence. Many men who sexually abuse their daughters are also guilty of beating their wives and children. At times one child may be singled out for repeated unwarranted punishment, while other siblings are spared.

One of the reasons incest may not be evident to outsiders is that the fathers often tend to restrict their violence to the home. These men realize that their wives and children will not present strong opposition to their rule. As a result, they have an ideal setting in which to indulge their appetite for domination. When such men do become involved in confrontations with other men who are their equals, however, they tend to be submissive and usually give in.

In many instances a father's initial sexual advances toward his daughter may be triggered by a traumatic family event. Often the crisis is connected with the abuser's relationship with his spouse. Among the most common "triggers" are the wife's death, her serious or extended illness, a divorce, or any event that makes her less accessible to her husband.

At times the triggering incident or separation may be less clear-cut. The wife may simply be away from home more than in the past. This could be because she has taken a job, becomes involved in volunteer work, or perhaps just works more hours at a job she's had for years.

Another type of trauma that often triggers incest is associated with the father's self-esteem. For example, the primary breadwinner may see the loss of a job as a severe blow to his ego. In fact, there is some evidence that the incidence of incest may be correlated to unemployment statistics.[5] This is certainly true of one Chicago neighborhood where, over a period of several years, the rate of child sexual abuse rose and fell with the unemployment rates.[6]

In some instances there is a correlation between the sexual abuse of children and the use of alcohol. In response to problems with their wives or jobs, some abusers may drink heavily. Alcohol tends to lessen inhibitions, and this can pave the way to incest. Approximately 65 percent of all incest victims claim that their fathers were drinking at the time of the first occurrence.[7] More recently, marijuana, cocaine, and even heroin have become more readily available, and reports of narcotic abuse by incestuous fathers have risen.

Very often abusive fathers try to isolate their victims from other family members or outsiders to whom the girls could go for help. The father may try to create barriers between the young girl and her mother by emphasizing how powerless the mother is or how little authority she actually wields within their home. This underscores the girl's perception of her mother as someone who is either unwilling or unable to help her.

Unfortunately, this often proves to be true. Sometimes a sexually abused girl is afraid to tell her mother because she thinks she may not be believed. Some mothers who find themselves in these situations go to great lengths to deny a very obvious reality. Often these mothers' first priority may be to maintain the status quo and keep the family intact.

Although the mother may be horrified at what she suspects, she may feel immobilized and powerless to act. Many mothers in incestuous families are women with passive personalities who are oppressed by dominating, patriarchal husbands. These women are usually extremely dependent on and subservient to their husbands. Many of them suffer from psychological or emotional difficulties and believe they'd be unable to survive on their own. Some may even fear their husband's physical retaliation if they dare to challenge his relationship to their daughter.

For these women the threat of losing their husbands and breaking up their families is worse than learning about the incest. They fear that taking the daughters' side may mean giving up the financial, physical, and emotional security provided by the men.

They may therefore attempt to preserve their

place in the family at any cost. If the price of maintaining the marriage includes closing their eyes to the sexual abuse of their own daughters, they may find it necessary to do so. Such women feel that they have to side with their husbands, as they believe that their first duty is to be loyal wives. Often these mothers are socially isolated, overburdened by caring for a number of small children, and economically dependent on their husbands. In general, they feel ill equipped to challenge their husbands' domination in any area.

The incestuous father may make it easy for the mother to side with him against the child. Often he denies the girl's accusations and tries to convince his wife that he's telling the truth. Often these women are extremely anxious to believe their spouses and thereby be spared all the pain and humiliation of what is actually happening.

If the case has already come to the attention of the authorities and the child is believed despite the protests of her parents, the girl's mother may use guilt to try to make her daughter say she lied about her father. A mother with divided loyalties may even try to make the child feel responsible for what happened. She may tell her daughter that the girl is destroying the family, or that everything was fine before she started spreading those horrible lies. But despite outward appearances, everything was never fine: not for the family, and certainly not for the sexually abused daughter.

In most instances fathers do not need to use force in persuading their daughters to go along with their desires. It is very difficult for a little girl to refuse her daddy's wishes. However, sexual encounters between parents and children always involve coercion on some level by the parent. The adult holds the position of power in the family. There is no way in which a child can realistically be in control or genuinely exercise free choice.

Children are, in a sense, captives within the family. They are likely to take their parents' threats seriously. Fearful of being abandoned or rejected, children feel compelled to go along with adults' demands. They often obey even though such actions make them feel guilty, frightened, or ashamed of their own bodies.

Many female incest victims take on the role of the traditional homemaker or wife within their household. This is especially true in situations where the mothers are incapacitated or absent for a period of time. For example, when Cheryl Pierson was only ten years old and her mother became ill, Cheryl was called on to help with the household chores and care for her baby sister. She also spent more and more time with her father.[8]

This common mother-daughter role reversal may also serve to inadvertently prolong the incestuous relationship. As the daughter evolves into the "miniature mother" of the family, her father may view her satisfaction of his own sexual demands as part of her role. And as the daughter assumes the responsibility of keeping the family intact, it may become even more difficult for her to report the incest. She may fear that her accusations will result in her father's being sent to jail and the family's being broken up.

Such an exchange of roles between mother and daughter may be extremely destructive to the young girl's normal development. She becomes burdened with excessive responsibilities at too early an age and is robbed of appropriate experiences with her peers, which are crucial to her growth into adulthood.

Parents who sexually abuse their children offer a variety of excuses for their actions. Many fathers try to hold to the delusion that they have the right to initiate their daughters into sexual activities. Some even assert that their actions were educational, telling the girls that they were preparing them for marriage or teaching them the facts of life.

At times incestuous fathers have even gone so far as to suggest that their young daughters were temptresses who actually seduced them. While it is true that children do have sexual feelings and do seek attention and affection from adults, it is the adult's responsibility to respond to the child's feelings and gestures in an appropriate manner. Exploiting the child for the parent's own sexual gratification is unacceptable.

Many incestuous relationships continue for some time. A father may interact sexually with his daughter at every available opportunity. In spite of the daughter's reluctance, it is not uncommon for an incestuous bond to continue for three years or longer. Many a man who commits incest finds sexually abusing his daughter more gratifying than having an extramarital affair with an adult woman. Having sex with his child tends to make the sexually abusive father feel strong and powerful. As the girl is often a virgin with little or no experience, the father need not feel that his performance as a sexual partner is being judged or evaluated unfavorably in comparison to that of others.

In addition, the father's sexual satisfaction may be intensified by indulging in a secret and forbidden act. In some cases, the child's unhappiness and feelings of oppression may serve to increase the father's sexual excitement. Incest, like numerous other sex crimes, is actually an exercise in power and domination. Feeling that he can master and rule another individual may be even more gratifying to the aggressor than any sexual pleasure derived from intercourse.

Some incestuous relationships go on until either the father dies or the girl leaves home. In most instances, however, incestuous relationships tend to end during the girl's teenage years. Usually it is the victim who insists that it must stop.

By the time the girl has reached high school, she often has become aware of the fact that what has been going on between her and her father is far more than just their "special secret." She understands now that she has been involved in a forbidden and illegal relationship. The sexually abused teenager finds that her feelings and sexual experiences differ vastly from those of her friends, who are worried about how far to go with a boy on the first date. Their questions about virginity don't apply to her. She's been having sex with her father for years and feels increasingly uncomfortable about it.

However, ending an incestuous relationship is not an easy task. If the girl appeals to her father to end it and there are other daughters in the family, he may let her go and initiate a sexual relationship with one of her sisters. The wish to protect a younger sister may make a girl continue to give in. If the girl is an only child or if her sisters are still too young to appeal to him, it may be even more difficult for her to escape.

As the girl struggles to free herself both sexually and emotionally from her father's grasp, her father may in turn become even more possessive. At this point, many incestuous fathers become overinvolved in their daughters' lives. They may attempt to regulate the amount of homework and housework required of the girl and to control all her spare time.

Often the victim's father may be particularly interested in curtailing her associations with boys. The abuser is trying to show his daughter that he's still in control of the situation. However, the restrictions he places on his daughter's life only serve to deepen her desperation and rage over what's happened.

If the father still refuses to stop, in most cases the young girl either tells someone the truth about what's been happening or runs away from home. It is not uncommon for an incest victim to feel that the only way to escape her intolerable situation is to find another powerful male figure. A great number of these girls become pregnant without marrying or marry at an unusually early age.[9] Often such girls see marriage as their ticket to freedom. However, some incest victims, like Cheryl Pierson, have seen violence as the only way out of an ugly situation that has dominated their lives for years.

At times it may be the incest victim who dies as the result of trying to break off the relationship. That's what happened to Sarah Ann Rairdon, a thirteen-year-old who disappeared on the four-mile walk from her rural Minnesota school to her home. The people of Otter Tail County formed a search party, and after a time the young girl's decomposed body was found in a pasture.

Meanwhile, her father, a thirty-eight-year-old tire repairman, had even gone on television to plead with the girl's abductor not to harm her. Three months later he confessed to her murder.

John Rairdon told police that he had been having sex with his daughter for nearly five years when she told him she wanted to break it off. The day before her death, Sarah Ann had successfully fought him off for the first time.

The next day her father picked her up at school and drove to an abandoned farmhouse, where he again tried to have intercourse with his daughter.

When she resisted, he stabbed her repeatedly in a rage. He watched Sarah Ann bleed to death and then hid her body in a barn until he had an opportunity to bury it.

Although a few months later John Rairdon recanted his confession, claiming that he hadn't killed his daughter after all, he was unable to convince a jury of his innocence. He was convicted of his daughter's murder and sentenced to life in prison.[10]

These incidents reveal what the horror of incest can lead to—the horror that hundreds of thousands of young people throughout America live with every day of their lives.[11] As victims of an unspeakable crime, they are often too afraid or ashamed to speak out. As defense attorney Paul Gianelli said of the Cheryl Pierson case, "It all fell in the lap of a sixteen-year-old. And it was a problem that finally proved too much to bear."[12]

CHAPTER 5

THE NEW UNDERGROUND RAILROAD

Unfortunately, many mothers in incestuous families feel too powerless to come to their children's aid. However, some women have stood up to end the abuse. Some have left their husbands. Others, already separated or divorced, have gone to court to restrain these fathers from further abusing the young victims during visitation periods.

In many instances, however, these mothers have found the courts unresponsive to their needs. One such well-known case involves Washington, D.C., plastic surgeon Elizabeth Morgan and her young daughter, Hillary. Dr. Morgan accused her ex-husband, Dr. Eric Foretich, a successful Virginia dentist, of sexually abusing their daughter. She supported her charges with both medical and psychological evidence.[1]

Dr. Foretich denied Morgan's accusations. To support his position he presented his own expert witnesses and a police polygraph examination that indicated his innocence.[2]

According to Elizabeth Morgan, a consulting child psychiatrist asserted that Dr. Foretich should not be permitted further visitation privileges with his daughter. She found the evidence of sexual abuse to be "clear and convincing."[3] The courts were not persuaded, however, and permitted continued unsupervised visits with little Hillary.

Elizabeth Morgan refused to obey the court. Instead, she hid her five-year-old daughter and would not disclose the child's whereabouts to the judge. Morgan did what she believed she had to do, but her decision was not without great personal cost. Because she refused to comply with the court order, Elizabeth Morgan was sent to jail. The court also seized her home and her passport. She was fined $200,000 and ordered to pay her ex-husband's legal fees as well. Dr. Morgan's surgical practice had to be closed. Her legal and medical debts, which amounted to more than $1.5 million, bankrupted her.[4]

Elizabeth Morgan's case is not unusual. Her experiences have been shared by many women across America.

Among them is Faye Yager, who claims that in 1971 she saw her ex-husband, Roger Jones, molest their eighteen-month-old daughter, Michelle. Although Yager went to court to gain full custody of her daughter, a jury awarded custody to the child's father.[5]

At that point, Yager took her daughter and fled.

While she was in hiding with the toddler, she learned that her daughter had contracted gonorrhea. Thinking that the courts would regard the child's sexually transmitted disease as proof of molestation, Yager returned to court. She hoped to win custody of her daughter, but instead she was jailed for having defied the first court order.

Custody of the child was awarded to her husband's parents, and Roger Jones continued to have access to his daughter. Since that time the little girl, Michelle, has grown up. It was later revealed that her father has been sought by both state and federal authorities for questioning in two molestation cases in California.[6]

In order to help mothers and abused children who find themselves in a position like hers, Faye Yager has now become the director of an organization called Mothers Against Raping Children. Yager's group helps to hide hundreds of children, their mothers, siblings, and in some cases their step-fathers. From her Atlanta home, she works closely with clusters of other people who are anxious to do whatever they can to assist sexually abused young people. Volunteers in more than thirty other states help to provide a safety net for desperate mothers and children, creating a highly effective network informally known as the "new underground railroad."

Children's advocates and sociologists estimate that there are thousands of mothers on the run in the United States. How many are being helped and supported by the new underground railroad is unclear, but within the first four months of just one year, Yager claims to have hidden more than one hundred children and their mothers.[7]

Many of the network organizers are mothers like Yager, women who at one time or another have accused their husbands of sexual abuse but have not found satisfaction within the court system. Today more and more mothers are "going underground." They reluctantly choose this alternative rather than accede to a court order that would allow their husbands, who have sexually abused their daughters, to have the right to visit or take custody of the child.

One woman who recently fled with her daughter from a court order in a southern city had to give up her career plans, her house, her car, and her support payments to do so. It wasn't the way she had hoped to safeguard her daughter, but after the court hearing, she felt she had no other choice. She explained, "I'm giving up all this because I love that child more than anything on earth."[8]

Although the new underground railroad may seem informal in its structure, these organizations are extremely adept in many areas. For example, in some instances, sympathetic physicians have provided false birth certificates to help runaway mothers and their children establish new identities. These birth certificates have enabled the women to acquire new driver's licenses and both mothers and children to apply for passports, social security numbers, all the necessary documents with which to start a new life.

In a few instances, volunteers have smuggled women and their children out of the country when the circumstances warranted it. One wealthy underground railroad volunteer housed a mother and her children in her vacation home in Mexico; another used her retreat in Canada for the same purpose. However, less extreme measures often suffice. Sometimes a woman just needs some help in making a quick escape. A bit of extra money, an apartment, and a job waiting for her in another state are usually all that are required for these often very resourceful women to begin their new lives.

The new underground railroad is rapidly expanding across America. For many women on the run, it's a safe haven during a fearful and stormy time in their lives. For some people, however, the railroad presents serious legal and ethical questions.

These people argue that when a mother defies a court order and goes "underground," she is in fact breaking the law. Even those who are sympathetic to what these women and their daughters have gone through do not always feel comfortable defying the legal system and engaging in activities that are often punishable by both fines and imprisonment. As David Lloyd of the National Center for Missing and Exploited Children stated, "We have no doubt that in most of the cases, the child has been subjected to abuse, but we are a nation of laws and people should obey them."[9]

The issue of skirting the law is especially troublesome to critics who fear that women who falsely charge their husbands with sexual abuse of their child might play on the sympathy of the new underground railroad volunteers. If these women were assisted in their flight, innocent men may lose all contact with their children and perhaps never be able to locate their offspring.

Vocal fathers' rights groups assert that the numbers of untrue allegations have risen significantly in recent years. Yet underground railroad volunteers claim that they've been made painfully aware of injustices and are continually on the alert for phony stories from women who simply wish to use their children to punish their husbands. Recalling their own experiences, women like Faye Yager insist that the underground railroad may be the only reasonable hope for sexually abused children.[10]

Many experts agree that the courts have not always been on target in instances of child sexual abuse.[11] It is extremely difficult, and in some cases nearly impossible, to determine sexual abuse in young children. Many judges who are not well versed in the effects of sexual abuse still require tangible irrefutable evidence before ruling against a father.

This is especially true of cases involving wealthy or middle-class men who may not fit the judges' preconceived notions of what a child molester looks like. As a result, many little girls may be sent back to the men who raped or molested them.

A recent study of allegations of sexual abuse in custody cases revealed that deliberately false allegations are "rarities."[12] Yet the American Bar Association reports that roughly half of all reported sexual abuse allegations in custody cases are ruled unfounded. This occurs because in all but the most blatant instances, these claims are "difficult to validate."[13]

Other aspects of the new underground railroad remain deeply disturbing. Many psychologists and child advocates stress that hiding a child may only worsen an already difficult situation.[14] They believe that children who are forced to live as fugitives may develop psychological disorders. Such young people are at risk of becoming socially alienated. However, mothers who have resorted to using the new underground railroad firmly believe that protecting their children from further sexual abuse is more important. If this avenue offers the only channel for their children's safety, they are grateful that it exists.

One mother who enlisted the help of the new underground railroad to save her four-year-old daughter from a sexually abusive situation had for two years been unsuccessful in trying to convince the courts that her daughter had been molested by the girl's father. She had secured documented evidence of injuries to her daughter as well as statements from the little girl citing her father as her abuser. But a number of family-court judges continued to allow the father unsupervised visitation periods with his daughter.

The girl's mother felt she had no choice but to obey the court's order. But when her child returned home with her genitals bruised after a week-long visit with her father, the woman immediately reported the incident to the police.

However, the father claimed that he had never abused his daughter and that these unfounded allegations were generated by his ex-wife, whom he described as "emotionally disturbed." According to the father, the young girl's genitals had become bruised while horseback riding.

The district attorney's office decided not to press charges against the father, stating that there wasn't sufficient evidence. In addition, the mother was informed that her daughter might have to be placed in a foster home until the disputes between her and her former husband were finally resolved.

At that point the woman decided to flee with her preschool daughter. She felt unable to deliver her child to the girl's father for still another visitation period as the court order required her to do. Instead, she took her daughter to her family's home in another state. There the child had a thorough medical examination, which revealed that she had contracted a sexually transmitted disease called condyloma.

Upon hearing this, the girl's father suggested that his daughter could have picked up the infection from a toilet seat, though there are no known instances of contracting condyloma in that manner. And once again, the mother found no redress from the courts.

Her only thought was to protect her daughter, and she realized that she'd have to go as far away as possible to do so. She had learned that her former husband had hired a private detective to find them, so she knew there was no time to waste.

This woman realized that she'd have to give up a great deal to embark on a life on the run. At the time she set out, she had almost no money left. She also had no idea of how difficult life on the road with a four-year-old could be. However, mother and child were eventually put in touch with a contact from the underground railroad. They were instructed to travel to the state of Wyoming. From there they were given the telephone number of a contact in the South. Their southern contact told them to give her twenty-four hours to make arrangements. The next day she said that if they could make it to Michigan, she'd be able to help them with some cash and temporary lodgings.

So the mother and daughter set out on a long and tiring journey to their new destination. Since they were unable to afford motels, the two slept in their car most nights.

Once they reached the Midwest, they actually

saw the various mechanisms of the new underground railroad in action. Their contact from the South didn't know where they'd be staying. She had just acted as a liaison to put them in touch with others who took over the arrangements from there. Confidentiality was crucial for everyone's protection. After speaking to a number of volunteers, the mother and daughter were introduced to a woman in her late sixties who put them up for the night.

Their hostess, a "key master" in the new underground railroad, was an exceptionally dedicated volunteer. She was anxious to do everything possible to stop the sexual abuse and exploitation of children, and was in the process of opening a 27,000-square-foot home for abused children. This helpful volunteer was already too familiar with the horrors of abuse. She had been sexually abused by her father every day from the time she was in the fourth grade until she turned eighteen.

That night marked only one of many stops on the woman's journey on the new underground railroad. Always on the lookout for police and private detectives, she and her daughter became expert at looking inconspicuous and altering their appearance. Both mother and daughter cut and dyed their hair. The little girl learned that when they were in a hotel room, she must not answer the door or look out the window.

Sometimes they stayed in inexpensive hotels, other times they were put up in isolated country homes. Once they stayed in very cramped quarters with a family of seven. But wherever they went, they found volunteers who were firmly committed to their cause. The mother and daughter hope that soon they can stop running from state to state and start to build a new life for themselves.

Those who travel the new underground railroad do not enjoy a comfortable existence. They don't know where they'll stay from day to day, whether their car will hold up on the journey, or whether they'll run out of money. But having rescued their children from abusive situations makes the trip worth it for most of these "passengers."

The new underground railroad has also been rewarding to many of the volunteer key masters who offer some hope to desperate people on the run. One such couple who have five children of their own have put up travelers on numerous occasions. They manage to make space by opening pull-out sofas and giving their own children makeshift beds or blankets on the floor.

Although they acknowledge that working as part of the new underground railroad may sometimes be crowded and inconvenient, they willingly make the necessary sacrifices. Like so many of the people involved with the network, this family has come face to face with child sexual abuse: The woman's daughter from a previous marriage had been sexually abused by her biological father. Although that ended more than four years ago, the teenage girl is still trying to deal with the anguish she experienced.

Despite the fact that this couple are not affluent, they are building a small house for the visiting fugitive families. They believe that what they do benefits not only abused children but their own family as well. It is important to them that their children not grow up to be self-centered, but instead learn to be caring and giving. For these new underground railroad volunteers, that's what life is about.

6

THE EFFECTS OF ABUSE

WHAT happens to a young person who has been repeatedly abused over a period of months or years? Assaults on children and teenagers have included beatings with straps, baseball bats, electric cable, or just plain fists.

In some instances, young people have been pursued by a parent with a loaded gun or other weapon. Following a severe beating, one girl hid in a corn field overnight with her little sister to avoid being shot by their enraged father.

A boy had a loaded pistol pointed at his head by his mother for over five hours. The boy felt certain that his mother would have killed both him and herself if a caseworker from Child Protective Services hadn't arrived at their apartment. Ironically, the caseworker's monthly visit just happened to fall at that time.[1]

The nature and extent of the abuse inflicted on the young person may vary according to the child's age and physical stature. The physical or emotional abuse of teenagers is often different from the mistreatment of young children. The very fact that the victim is an adolescent or young adult makes it so.

ADOLESCENT ABUSE

A teenager's mental abilities and emotional makeup are likely to be more advanced than those of a young child. An adolescent tends to reason much more like an adult than a child does, and as a result the interaction between parents and teenagers becomes considerably more complex. The adolescent's physical power also is significantly greater than that of a young child. If the adolescent is assaulted by his parent, he may have the capacity to strike back with a forceful blow.

In addition, the adolescent has many more resources available to him that may influence parental conflicts in positive or negative ways. For example, the adolescent has been around other families and adults. By this time he has some idea of what he does or does not deserve and what society at large deems appropriate behavior on his part and on the part of his parents. At this stage of his development, he is capable of bringing such comparisons into the conflict with his parent.

Many teenagers also become sophisticated enough to know what behavior on their part will trigger violent or aggressive behavior in their parent. These triggers can be pulled by the teenager at significant times to embarrass either the parent or himself. Such actions only tend to intensify an already explosive family situation, but they take place nevertheless.

Adolescents have a considerably broader range of relationships than children do with people outside the home. This plays a significant role in their lives. They may form close bonds with friends, teachers, aunts or uncles, employers, or other members of the community.

Such relationships may create insecurity or jealousy in parents as they realize that they are no longer the only important adults in their children's lives. The normal development of boy-girl relationships during the teen years can be particularly upsetting to some parents because it brings up the possibility of sexual relations.

These new factors common to adolescence put stress on old family boundaries and methods of dealing with each other. Some parental behavior that was appropriate during their children's early youth is no longer appropriate during adolescence and may eventually explode into abuse.

Spanking a three-year-old has a different psychological implication than trying to spank a sixteen-year-old. The same degree of intimacy and physical contact deemed affectionate behavior with a toddler may carry sexual implications when a parent is dealing with a young person who is near or past puberty. It is necessary for a parent to oversee practically every aspect of a two-year-old's life; the same authoritarian approach in raising a teenager may signal overinvolvement of the parent.

Some abused adolescents were also abused as children. These young people simply continue to be victims. Others are abused for the first time as teenagers. In either instance, power is generally the basic issue underlying adolescent abuse. In our society, children have very little power over their own lives. However, adolescence brings the young individual a new sense of power as he becomes aware of his increased ability to perceive, act, and engage in arguments. Many teenagers deliberately challenge parental authority in various ways. Some parents treat their children's assertive behavior as a threat to their position.

A teenager in an abusive situation is faced with a serious dilemma. Even severely abused adolescents may experience anxiety and guilt when they are finally separated from their tormentors. They are told so often that they are worthless that many come to believe their powerful parent's distorted view of life. At times, abused teenagers' personal sense of worth and value has been so diminished that they may even come to believe the abuser's justifications for abusing them. They may wrongly feel that they actually deserve to be punished.

Because many abused adolescents have never lived away from home, they are often very dependent on the person who is abusing them and are unable to conceive of a successful life away or on their own. Fear of separation from the parental figure can paralyze whatever inner resources victims might have, and may lead them to deny their pain even to themselves. If the thought of breaking away is too frightening, victims may choose to minimize their own mistreatment rather than report it to the authorities.

Society tends to be highly sympathetic to very young abused children, but is not always as supportive of teenagers who have been abused. At times these young people are stereotyped as "behavior-problem teens" who provoked uncontrollable rage in their parents. Some people might even feel that such teenagers "got what was coming to them."

It is also often presumed that teenagers have the resources to leave their homes if they choose to do so. They are not regarded in the same way as an infant who has been beaten while lying helplessly in his crib. Actually, most adolescents are both financially and emotionally completely dependent on their parents. When an abused teenager, like an abused wife, does not take advantage of the assistance of outside agencies, he is often unfairly viewed as a contributor to the problem.

The experience of being abused varies markedly according to each situation. In addition, the effects of abuse on the victim differ depending on whether the younger person was first abused as a teenager or has been abused since early childhood. In some families, the level of conflict may first erupt into adolescent abuse over a particular issue or because the adolescent himself has introduced some new elements into the family relationship. The normal strivings of a teenager to define his sense of identity and self may be enough to enrage his parent. Sometimes this leads to inappropriate and abusive behavior as a means of trying to control him.

On the other hand, some abuse is linked to adolescence only by coincidence. In these instances, the abuse began in infancy or childhood and simply continued during the teen years. The abuse inflicted on the young person has nothing to do with his age or development into adulthood. It may seem unbelievable that any young person might have been mistreated for such a length of time without an outside agency intervening, but it happens quite often. This is particularly true in situations in which the abuse does not dramatically change or increase at any given point, but continues at the same level throughout the child's residence in the home.

Still another type of abuse of young people occurs when mild or moderate forms of corporal punishment escalate into abusive behavior. A person who was spanked as a child may find, now that he is an adolescent, that his parent has taken to beating him with a strap. This is common among parents who find it necessary to severely restrict their offspring's behavior in order to feel that they are still firmly in charge. Threatened by their teenager's increasing size, strength, and independence, these adults apply additional force in the name of discipline.

Normally, adolescence is a period for changing, growing, and seeking new forms of freedom and independence. The adolescent experiences biological, intellectual, and social changes that affect his life. It is a time when a person can try on adult roles and test how it feels to assert himself in many new and different ways. The disruption in family roles brought about by this testing can often serve to ignite the sparks of abuse.

The adolescent years mark a milestone in physical and sexual development for most human beings. Puberty signals the maturation of the sexual organs as well as such secondary sex characteristics as facial hair and a lower-pitched voice for boys and breast development and a widening of the pelvis in girls. The hormones that accompany such physical changes may also be responsible for mood fluctuations in many people. Such biological changes often go hand in hand with an increased interest in members of the opposite sex and with the initiation of dating as well. Such volatile issues as curfews, dating activities, friends, and the choice of dating partners may all affect relationships within the family.

The concept of teenage sexuality in any form can be extremely disturbing to many parents. In dealing with emotional issues such as chastity, trust, and a teenager's newly felt need to assert himself, emotions often flare—and abusive behavior may come into play.

Another change in the teenager with which a parent must learn to cope is the intellectual development that usually accompanies adolescence. The teen years bring an increased ability to ponder and deal with hypothetical problems. Adolescents learn to think abstractly about academic subjects as well as their own feelings, their parents, and their relationship to others.

Teenagers are often far less willing to automatically accept another person's point of view than young children are. Usually they are able to come up with an evaluation of matters on their own. This ability may enable a teenager to make a deeper analysis of his school studies; it also means that his parents will, perhaps for the first time in their lives, have to deal with a young person in their home who can think and reason independently of guidance. Many abusive parents find to their dismay that they are no longer able to mold their offspring's thinking to the extent that they might wish to.

Perhaps one of the most striking changes that accompany adolescence occurs in the realm of social development. Many teenagers may appear to be overly concerned with evaluation and acceptance by their friends or peer group. This new emphasis is actually an attempt by adolescents to separate from their parents and establish an identity of their own.

A teenager's circle of friends may greatly influence the way he dresses, what he eats, with whom he socializes, and how he spends his time both in and out of school. While at one time this young person might have tried to please his parents, now his efforts may be turned much more toward winning the approval of his friends. At times, the parents of a teenager may miss the esteem their child once held them in and may feel somewhat displaced by the teenager's friends.

In many instances, the abusive parent may feel that he is in competition with the adolescent's friends. A parent who is overly involved with his child may believe that the teenager's style of dress or his general appearance reflects the parent's success or failure as care taker. He may feel, unjustifiably, that he must control his adolescent's life more rigidly, even though it may be nearly impossible to closely monitor a teenager's activities away from home. The result may be highly charged disciplinary sessions that can lead to abuse.

Outside forces can bring further pressures to bear on families with adolescents. Being somewhere between child and adult, adolescents face limitations and restrictions in almost every area of their lives. In earlier times when people died at a significantly younger age, positions of respect were often accorded to young people. (In fact, many of the early settlers who came on their own to the New World were teenagers.) The frustration of not being taken seriously often contributes to tense family interactions.

Unfortunately, our society offers very few tangible guidelines that help to define clearly the adolescent's ascent into adulthood. Although there are age limitations set by law on the rights to vote, drive a car, or drink alcoholic beverages, it is often difficult for a parent to know just when his child is ready to take on new responsibilities. The differing views between parent and teenager regarding what is suitable behavior for an adolescent often explode into bitter disputes, which may lead to abuse.

OVERALL EFFECTS OF ABUSE

Children and adolescents are extremely adaptable beings; they can survive in a wide range of situations. Youths who live under hostile abusive conditions learn to adjust, in one way or another, to painful experiences. Unfortunately, over the course of time, an unhealthy environment damages an individual's development.

One danger is that children learn to become successful or unsuccessful adults by identifying with and imitating those who take care of them. Children become like their parents because of the emotional bonds between them. It is natural for children to copy the people who matter to them. Young people absorb whatever atmosphere they are exposed to, whether it is a warm and loving one or a distorted, violent one.

Feelings of guilt, shame, and fear are common among abused children. Some have stated that they had continual nightmares while they lived at home but that their bad dreams lessened after either their family situation improved or they were removed from the home.[2]

Often abused children develop bed-wetting problems as a result of their stressful home environment. If the stress in their lives is not lessened, the bed wetting may continue for a number of years.

This can be a serious source of anxiety for children in shelters and group homes for children. Some of them suffer from chronic insomnia because they force themselves to try to stay awake all night. They're afraid that if they fall asleep, they might be caught wetting their bed. One young boy handled the problem by pretending to go to bed when everyone else did. When he felt certain that the others were fast asleep, he'd sit up in bed and read comic books by flashlight.[3]

Children with high self-esteem are better able to handle challenges, express creativity and inventive thinking, and deal competently with various situations. A person with low self-esteem thinks poorly of himself and believes that he will fail. As a result of such thinking, the individual often does in fact fail. It is almost as if such a person's actions match his negative thinking and expectations. Children and adolescents with low self-esteem are more likely than others to display problem behavior in school and social settings, experience a high degree of anxiety, and act destructively toward objects and people.

Abused boys frequently get in trouble with school authorities because of rowdiness and open hostility to teachers and classmates. Both girls and boys from abusive homes are chronically truant. In many cases truancy is soon followed by dropping out of school. Many of these young people view self-destructive actions as their only way to deal with a chaotic family situation. One fourteen-year-old boy said he ran away because he had to get away from the fighting and beatings at home. He felt that starving or stealing to stay alive would be better than remaining with his parents.[4] Many abused children end up on the street as runaways and prostitutes.

Evidence of drug and alcohol abuse among battered young people is astoundingly high. Some start drinking heavily as early as nine years old. Abused children often use drugs as a buffer, looking to them as a temporary escape route from the violence they face on a daily basis.

Abused children often do not view attending school as a possible way to change their lives. School cannot provide them with prompt relief from their oppressive home problems. For some of these young people, school is little more than a place where they might be able to buy drugs.[5]

In some cases, abused children may find it especially difficult to relate to school authorities. In
April, 1977, the Supreme Court ruled in *Ingram* v
Wright to uphold corporal punishment in the
schools. According to the court decision, teachers
may "exercise powers of control, restraint, discipline, and correction as necessary, provided that
the discipline is reasonable." But abused young people may view strict teachers or those who use corporal punishment as extensions of their intolerable
home life.

A young person's anxiety over his aggressive feelings might result in violent expression of those
feelings. People who are anxious about aggression
often respond more aggressively than others to situations that may evoke such feelings.

Mistreatment tends to exaggerate a young person's uncertainty about himself and the world
around him. Another result of child abuse is a lack
of empathy in its victims. The ability to empathize
is the ability to place oneself in the circumstances
of another and feel what that person must be feeling. The phrase "walk a mile in my shoes" perhaps
best captures the meaning of empathy. The ability
to identify with another person's feelings and re-
sponses fosters a humane and forgiving society. People behave more responsibly when they are aware

of the effect their behavior will have on others.

An empathetic person is one who can be sympathetic and who at times will work hard in order to help another individual. The benefits of empathy, to both the individual and society at large, are numerous. Children who are empathetic score higher on academic tests than others do; an empathetic child tends to be less hostile and aggressive in school and social situations. Many people believe that empathy is the very cornerstone of morality in our society.

But many abused young people lose their ability to empathize at an early age, and some never develop it at all. Because they were never shown empathy while they were growing up, they exhibit the same lack of empathy their parents demonstrated to them. Many teenagers who have been abused respond to younger children in very much the same way their parents responded to them. They cannot identify with the child's needs.

Along with low self-esteem and a lack of empathy, feelings of rejection are common among abused young people. Parental rejection can make a young person extremely dependent on his friends and other adults. Those who do not know love and acceptance in their early years may seek it ferociously for much of their lives. Their search for acceptance, combined with their feelings of worthlessness, may often prime such individuals to become targets for mistreatment by other abusive people they may encounter.

These individuals do not perceive the treatment they receive as terrible—that is all they have ever known. In instances where they do realize that they are being treated badly, they often still do not break away. They firmly believe that they do not deserve any better. Abuse is reminiscent of their past, and they feel deserving of mistreatment. Abusive treatment may become the distinctive characteristic of the majority of their social relationships and interactions.

Such people are extremely vulnerable to hurt and rejection by others and may find it almost impossible to abandon the role of victim. For many abused youths, the major challenge of their lives becomes finding ways to escape the feelings of pain and humiliation that characterize their daily existence. Some turn to drugs and alcohol, others even attempt suicide. These are desperately unhappy children and young adults who see only very limited possibilities or none at all for a brighter future. Some of them see suicide as the only means of escaping the pain that dominates their lives.

Young abuse victims who attempt suicide or even

merely contemplate it are actually turning all their rage inward. Ninety-five percent of the abuse victims in a recent study stated that at one time or another they harbored fears about what they might do to themselves or a family member (usually the father) if their lives became unbearable.[6] These young people were afraid of themselves. They felt haunted by the terrible possibility that circumstances at home might drive them to murder or suicide or both.

Dr. Robert Sadoff, a clinical professor of psychiatry at the University of Pennsylvania, has extensively studied the phenomenon of children who strike out against and kill their parents (parricide). Dr. Sadoff believes the potential for parricide among children from violent homes is extremely high.

According to Dr. Sadoff, parricide doesn't happen immediately, but only becomes an option to a battered child after repeated traumas occur over a long period of time. The young person tries to find different ways of handling what's happening to him, then becomes frustrated and believes there's no way out. Feeling closed in and trapped, the person kills his abuser in an attempt to escape from the horror of his everyday life.[7]

In 1984 seventeen-year-old Robert Ludwig, Jr., killed his father, a Boston taxi driver, with six hatchet blows to the head. Yet friends and neighbors rallied to the defense of the boy, who received a suspended sentence of nine to fifteen years. A court-appointed psychiatrist testified that Ludwig's was the worst case of abuse he had ever seen.[8]

Although most children who are abused do not kill their parents, they frequently develop serious personality problems. Mistreated boys often express their rage over being abused in an aggressive or assaultive manner, such as drinking, brawling, or reckless driving, whereas young girls are more likely to turn the anger and hurt inward against themselves. This may reflect a culture that still strongly frowns on any expression of aggressiveness in females. Girls may run away from home or may become involved in alcohol or drug abuse, defying curfews, sexual promiscuity, and similar acts.

It is interesting to note that in very recent years aggressive delinquent acts committed by young women appear to be on the rise. As the restrictiveness of traditional roles becomes more relaxed, we may continue to see more of a shift in this direction. Still, regardless of the form a young person's destructive response to mistreatment takes, the problem of his or her abuse within the home remains.

The devastating effects of child abuse bear serious and dangerous consequences for all of society as well as for the youths themselves. There is a definite connection between extreme abuse and homicide.

An astonishing number of teenagers who have actually committed murder other than parricide were severely physically abused during their childhood. In addition, many well-publicized murders have been committed by individuals who were abused as children. Charles Manson, the cult leader responsible for the brutal murder of actress Sharon Tate and others, is only one example.

On May 15, 1972, a young man named Arthur Bremer attempted to assassinate Governor George Wallace of Alabama by shooting him. Fortunately, the governor lived. The recordings of court procedures, as well as files from several social agencies to which Bremer was known, revealed an early childhood background of neglect and violence.

On June 6, 1968, Sirhan B. Sirhan assassinated Senator Robert Kennedy. American journalists traced Sirhan's background and childhood in Palestine and discovered through neighbors' testimony that Sirhan's father frequently beat all of his children.

The effects of mistreatment are considerably more far-reaching than one might initially realize.

Abuse not only destroys the child victim but jeopardizes the foundation of a humane society.

Occasionally an abused child is fortunate. He escapes the maddening horror of his environment not just to survive but to thrive in a loving and enriching atmosphere. That's what happened to Michael. Michael met his second mother when he was still a small child. On the day before Mother's Day, Patricia Caporale had looked up to find her husband, Joe, standing in their bedroom doorway, holding a small, wide-eyed boy and a brown paper bag.

He placed the child on the bed next to his wife and introduced the child as their new son, Michael. Joe added that since the paper bag contained the only clothes Michael owned, she might want to go shopping for the boy soon.

At first Pat Caporale was stunned. She just looked at her husband and then at the child. Michael's hair and eyes were brown; for a moment he reminded her of a lost puppy. Pat's husband explained that three-year-old Michael was one of three brothers who'd been sexually abused and neglected by their natural mother. Michael had received the worst treatment. As a result, the child hadn't fared well. He was only about half the size a child of his age he should be.

The authorities had become aware of Michael's mother's mistreatment of her children and had threatened to remove them permanently from her home. Michael's mother gave the boys to an older woman who was her aunt. The aunt in turn had given the boys to Pat's brother and sister-in-law because she was aware that the couple had been trying for years to adopt a child. However, three poorly nourished children under the age of four who needed a great deal of attention proved to be too much for the couple. They asked Joe if he and Pat would raise Michael as their own.

As it turned out, Pat was glad that her husband had brought the young boy home. She and her husband had thought for some time about adopting a child who needed them. They discussed with their own son, Mark, the prospect of adopting Michael, and he agreed that Michael should become part of the family.

Turning Michael into a healthy, properly functioning child was not a simple task for the boy's new family. Michael was seriously malnourished. The lack of proper nutrition caused the young boy's stomach to protrude. Some of his normal development and growth processes had been stunted as well. At that point, Michael was unable to talk. The only word he could say was "boofs," which was what he called his shoes. The child was extremely attached to those shoes. Whenever they weren't on his feet, he kept them in close view.

The Caporales' family doctor examined Michael and came up with some disturbing findings. Tests revealed that there had been untreated broken bones in both Michael's legs and that permanent damage might have been done to his spine. The child suffered from serious malnutrition and delays in his mental development. Their physician warned the Caporales that he couldn't be certain that Michael would ever catch up, or even learn to talk, for that matter.

Despite all the odds against him, Pat and Joe were determined to turn Michael's life into a success story. They relied on love, hope, patience, and understanding to foster their new son's growth. There were frustrating periods, but Michael tried hard and in time things really began to improve. Within six months of his arrival at the Caporales', Michael was able to speak in simple sentences. Within two years he could speak well enough to enter kindergarten. In time, Michael came to excel in math and sports. Today he is doing well at his junior high school. The Caporales were so pleased with Michael that they decided to adopt another child in need.[9]

Unfortunately, the happy ending of Michael's story is more of an exception than a rule. Too few abused children are miraculously rescued as Michael was. Often there isn't any helpful outside intervention. As a result these young people may live with their childhood pain for years to come.

CHAPTER 7

FINDING
A SOLUTION

A seven-year-old boy from Los Angeles, California, had been beaten repeatedly by his parents for years. At times, to frighten and punish the boy, they'd drag him out to the backyard, where they'd bury him in a shallow grave. The boy's only access to air was a straw that poked through to the ground's surface.

One afternoon a neighbor overheard the little boy screaming and struggling as his parents tried to bury him. She called the police, and they rescued the child. A later medical examination revealed that the boy had suffered brain damage as a result of receiving insufficient oxygen during the times he had been buried.[1]

Four-year-old Dustin Akers resided in Shelby, Ohio, with his parents. Dustin might have been thought of as fortunate because his mother was an obstetrical nurse. However, Dustin's father abused him. On one occasion, his father shook Dustin so severely that the child was left blind and brain damaged. His father was charged with child endangerment. He was convicted and spent thirty days in jail.[2]

Children who are neglected and abused live in desperation. Often they suffer their torment silently, too afraid or ashamed to speak to anyone about what is really happening to them. The myriad horror stories of child abuse underscore the truth: that in too many instances the safeguards that are supposed to protect these children have failed them.

In response to this national tragedy, the following legislation has been enacted to provide further protection for young people.

■ The Child Abuse Prevention Act of 1974 was the first federal legislation on child maltreatment. It established the National Center for Child Abuse and Neglect in Washington, D.C., to provide research, guidelines, and information on the prevention of child abuse.

■ The Adoption Assistance and Child Welfare Act of 1980: States are required to offer support services to families before removing a child from the home. If removal is necessary, a specific plan for the child while he is in foster care must be established and reviewed every six months. A child can become eligible for adoption after eighteen months if the family cannot be reunited.

■ Reporting laws: At present all states and U.S. territories require professionals working with children to report suspected child abuse and neglect.

■ The Child Protection Act of 1984: This legislation raises the age limit in child pornography cases from sixteen to eighteen, increases fines for offenders, and specifies that any sexually explicit pictures of children constitute pornography.

■ The Child Support Enforcement Amendments of 1984: States are required to withhold wages from parents who are delinquent in child-support payments.

Unfortunately, often legislation to protect children is only as effective as the financial resources allotted to ensure its enforcement. In many instances, funding to protect children has been woefully inadequate. According to Susan Robinson of the National Conference of State Legislatures, the greatest obstacle to saving children at risk of abuse is a lack of money for effective preventive measures.[3] Unfortunately, many children are not eligible for help or don't even come to the attention of the authorities until after they've been in serious danger.

Another factor that acts against children in abusive situations is that currently too many different agencies operate independently of one another. For example, an abusive father who has also been arrested for theft to support his drug habit may be known to the police. At the same time a school counselor may be working with the man's son, who has been displaying behavior problems at school. The counselor may be forced to function with limited or distorted information about the child's actual home life. Although both agencies, the police and the school system, are aware of this potentially high-risk family, it often takes a serious tragedy before they come together to see what measures might have been taken.

The fact that child abuse is monitored on a county level rather than on a state level also hinders intervention efforts. Families are frequently on the move. A parent who's been apprehended for child abuse in one county can simply move to another county in the same state where there is no record of his prior problems.

At this time there is no national child-welfare reporting system. Therefore, as records are not centrally stored, reporting remains inconsistent and uneven. It is nearly impossible to track down an abusive family if they frequently change their residence.

Unfortunately, even when cases of child abuse reach the courts, the burden of proof generally lies with the child. If the prosecutor fails to present his case against the abusive parent forcefully, usually the judge simply returns the child to the troubled home. Many child advocates have stressed the importance of judges' becoming better trained in obtaining information from children. Yet at the present time, such training is nonexistent.

To worsen matters, abusive parents who kill their children usually receive very light sentences. This is because it is nearly impossible to prove that the murder was premeditated in such instances. Jurors are reluctant to believe that people can deliberately kill their own children. A tearful parent who swears that his child's death was a tragic accident (he only meant to discipline the child) generally will not be dealt with harshly. Individuals who severely maim or abuse their children also are rarely subjected to stiff sentences. A man from Seattle, Washington, who repeatedly used an electric cattle prod on all of his children served only six months in jail.

What can be done to change things? Most child-abuse prevention experts are in favor of establishing widespread education programs in schools across the country. By 1987 approximately twenty-five percent of the nation's elementary schools had implemented this type of curriculum.[4] The goal of such programs is to convince abused young people that they are not to blame for what has happened and to assure them that they don't deserve to be mistreated. The children are taught that sometimes their parents aren't right and that violence has no place in a home. They are also encouraged to tell someone when they are victimized by their parents or caregivers.

In addition, nearly seventeen percent of the hospitals with maternity services offer educational and support programs for new parents. These programs are important, for in many cases the new parents are teenagers or not much older and have little or no background in effective child-rearing techniques. It is hoped that the number of programs will increase.

Perhaps one of the most important new trends in combating child abuse is combining the resources of schools, law-enforcement personnel, child-welfare bureaus, and mental-health agencies. In this team approach, the key is effective interagency cooperation and coordination. When the various agencies are able to work together on cases that involve domestic violence, the chance of abused children being lost in the shuffle is significantly lessened.

This kind of cooperation is essential if children's lives are to be saved. For example, Flora Colao, a social worker who offers abuse-prevention programs aimed at children, had worked at PS 41 in New York City until the spring of 1986. There she taught children how abuse differs from discipline and where to go for help if it happened to them. However, some of the teachers and parents felt that the program was unnecessary in a neighborhood as lovely as theirs. As a result the program was discontinued. The following fall Lisa Steinberg entered PS 41, and a year and a half later she was dead.

Some people believe that multidisciplinary groups, including people in medicine, mental health, social work, and law, should be working together on the front lines to intervene in high-risk family situations. Child advocate Dr. Vincent Fontana has stressed the importance of breaking through the bureaucracy where child abuse is concerned. He feels that a separate department for children needs to be established on either a city or state level. In addition, Dr. Fontana believes that the department's head must have direct access to either the mayor or the governor.[5]

Today child-abuse experts are encouraging all members of the community to become more involved in keeping children safe. They feel it's important to regard children not as other people's property but rather as everyone's responsibility. For example, Dr. Eli Newburger of Boston's Children's Hospital advocates that all adults should look out for all children.[6]

The following signs may be important indicators

that a child is being abused or neglected at home.

■ Physical injuries (such as blackened eyes, badly bruised bodies, broken bones) for which no plausible explanation is given.

■ A child who seems unduly distracted or demonstrates an unusual absence of alertness.

■ An obvious lack of necessary medical care.

■ A child who is usually dirty, unkempt, or inappropriately dressed.

■ A child's demonstrated fear of his parents and a reluctance to return to his home.

■ A child who bullies younger or weaker children (the child may often be copying his parents' behavior).

Even one person can make a difference. Intervention by someone outside the child's family may be the only hope for an abused young person whose life could be in danger. Yet in too many instances people are reluctant to become involved. Feeling that it's none of their business, neighbors or others may hesitate to call the police or a social-service agency.

Following Lisa Steinberg's death, a New York City Board of Education report showed that eight people on her school's staff had noticed Lisa's unkept hair and clothing. At least five people had seen bruises on the young girl. Still, although there had been reports from other individuals, no one from the school had ever reported these possible signs of abuse to the proper authorities.

Unfortunately, however, sometimes even reporting the abuse may not save the child. Child-welfare workers in New York and other cities are overwhelmed by the number of cases for which they are responsible. Under such circumstances some children fall between the cracks. Federal, state, and local funding doesn't begin to approach what's needed to make a genuine dent in the problem. As a result, underpaid workers struggle with unrealistically heavy case loads.[7]

According to professional social-work standards, a normal case load should be between twenty and twenty-five dockets. In actuality, however, many caseworkers are expected to oversee between thirty and fifty cases, and in some areas this number is significantly higher.[8]

In addition, caseworkers are often poorly trained for their jobs. Many of them have just graduated from college. Yet within days of becoming caseworkers, they may find themselves on the front lines of life-and-death situations. Having to function in a difficult and demanding position, many of them quit; there's often a rapid turnover rate in their field.[9]

In a few places, state and local agencies have taken measures to help social workers improve their on-the-job performance. Children's protective service workers in Wisconsin can now participate in an eight-day intensive training program. Metro Ministries in Corpus Christi, Texas, created a program called Adopt a Child Abuse Caseworker. Under this system, thirty-five caseworkers are matched up with various churches in the area. The congregations work with the caseworkers to supply necessary support services for needy young people.

A third program in Aurora, Colorado, trains teachers and caseworkers to detect the early signs of child abuse. At times these signs may be as subtle as a talkative child who suddenly becomes quiet and withdrawn. The program has been effective; officials claim that the number of reports of child abuse has dramatically increased.

Unfortunately, even when child-abuse situations have been identified, there are often no readily available clear-cut solutions. Historically, society has operated under the assumption that if the child is removed from an abusive home, everything will be all right. However, where to place these children is a problem.

There is currently a serious shortage of available foster homes. This may be due partly to the fact that with fewer two-parent homes in America, fewer families feel able to take children in. In some areas, the shortage has become acute. Gordon Johnson, director of the Illinois Department of Children and Family Services, has urgently pleaded for one thousand more people to become foster parents in order to prevent the present system from collapsing throughout the state.

However, simply recruiting more foster parents may not solve the problem. Reports of child abuse within the foster-parent system have repeatedly come to the attention of officials. Some foster parents are unqualified for the job they're expected to do; others become overwhelmed by the multiple problems that often come with the children they take in.

Often foster parents find themselves in extremely stressful situations. Professor Emily Jean McFadden of Eastern Michigan University feels that because of the present shortage of foster families, caseworkers tend to overload the existing ones with children in need. Often these foster parents try their best to cope under pressure, but sometimes something finally snaps.[10]

Things can become difficult even for the best-intentioned foster parents. For example, one foster family refused to keep an eight-year-old girl with them after she killed a kitten. The girl, who'd been sexually abused by her biological father, refused to wear underwear and continually exposed herself on the school bus.[11]

Foster parents face numerous challenges in their role. They must maintain a firm balance between providing love and care for the child and becoming overly attached. Foster care was designed as a temporary solution. According to the American Public Welfare Association, over half of the more than 250,000 children placed in foster care each year are eventually united with their natural families. Another ten percent are adopted.[12]

Foster parents also suffer from what is generally regarded as a negative public image. Often they are viewed as taking in children only for the money. Although this may be true of some such parents, social workers stress that often the money is barely sufficient to cover the costs of food and clothing for the young person.[13]

Usually people become foster parents because they want to do something to help children in need. As Jim Lardie, president of the Association of Child Advocates, described them, "The vast majority of foster parents see this as part of their life's work.

They say that this is what they were put on earth to do."[14] In fact, a placement with a loving, supportive family can be among the most beneficial experiences in a troubled child's life. One psychotherapist described his evaluation of two children who'd been placed in an excellent foster home this way: "Living in a solid family setting was more therapeutic than weekly counseling sessions."[15]

In addition to handling troubled and disturbed young people, foster parents must negotiate their way through the multileveled bureaucracy of the child-welfare system. Many of these understaffed agencies cannot offer foster parents the training programs and support services necessary to enable them to adequately perform their duties. Some experts have advocated a more specialized foster-care system in which certain families would be trained to handle children with specific physical or emotional difficulties. Theodore Stein, a professor of social policy at the State University of New York, has suggested a multilayered foster-care program in which certain foster parents would be trained to take in children for short-term stays, while others would be involved with children for extended periods.[16]

However, some child-care professionals believe the answer lies in trying to keep families together.

They feel that the focus should be shifted from rescuing the child to rescuing the family. Since most American children grow up within their own families, abused children could feel more "like everyone else" if they were able to remain at home. Most families, even those in which severe abuse has occurred, want to find a way to stay together. This might be partly accomplished through intensive one-on-one counseling with a qualified social worker who makes frequent home visits.

A private agency in Washington called Homebuilders does this type of work with approximately five hundred families a year. Ninety-five percent of the families that received treatment there showed a marked decrease in domestic violence. Eighty-five percent of these families reported improved communication skills among family members.[17]

Short-term intervention with violent families has also been extremely beneficial in some areas. Child advocate Dr. Vincent Fontana operates a crisis nursery at New York City's Foundling Hospital. Parents are able to leave their children there for a few nights if they feel they are about to lose control. Parents who use the facility are able to get relief from a high-stress situation without being made to feel ashamed. One twenty-five-year-old mother described why she brought her daughters to the center one evening: "I didn't know what to do. I never hit my children, but I got tense."[18]

Another important innovation is Childhaven, a five-day-a-week treatment and enrichment program for abused children. Each day a Childhaven van picks the children up and later returns them to their families. These stops allow Childhaven personnel to be aware of how things are going within the home. For example, if the mother is having a difficult morning, Childhaven workers can help get the children dressed as well as encourage the mother to come in to the center for counseling.

In addition to caring for children, Childhaven offers support services for the parents. Many of the mothers involved in the program are single parents who have been victims of violence themselves. Parents are invited to join a parents' group at the center. The groups work to make the participants more competent parents. Mothers are taught improved communication skills to use with their children as well as how to cope better with stress.

Another group that has been of great help to troubled parents is the self-help organization Parents Anonymous. The basis of the organization is the premise that people facing similar dilemmas can pool their resources and work together to help themselves, their children, and other group members.

At PA, parents have an opportunity to share their feelings with others who have had similar experiences. In such a group the members need not fear the judgment and condemnation of people who may not fully understand all the circumstances that led to their abusive behavior.

PA provides an opportunity for member parents to let off steam as stress accumulates. The members may exchange phone numbers; if a parent feels that the inner turmoil he is experiencing may explode into violence against his child, he can call another member to "talk out" his feelings. Experienced PA members help new parents to become acclimated to the program, and these new members then become responsible for other newcomers.

PA teaches abusive parents that it's all right to ask for help. Parents are encouraged to learn to deal with their negative feelings, as well as to redirect destructive tendencies into constructive channels.

There are no waiting lists or red tape in Parents Anonymous. A crisis need not erupt for a parent in trouble to receive the aid and support of the other group members. New members are welcomed into the group at any time. There are over twelve hundred chapters of PA throughout America. The group's goal is to reach the many thousands of parents who may never make newspaper headlines, but who need help nevertheless.

Protective legislation, innovative programs, and self-help groups for parents and families have been important steps in combating child abuse. However, the war to protect children has hardly been won. Child abuse in America continues to be a growing problem.

EPILOGUE

ON a cold February evening in Newark, New Jersey, a three-year-old girl and her eleven-month-old brother were supposedly being cared for by their fifty-one-year-old grandmother. Unfortunately, the grandmother left the two children alone in her home with four massive Rottweiler dogs.

Once the children were by themselves, two of the four dogs attacked the little girl, ripping her scalp off. She was also bitten on her face, arms, and legs. The child was taken to the hospital, where she was in guarded condition. When her father saw her there, he reported that the small girl wasn't able to speak to him, but instead just kept crying. The grandmother was arrested shortly after the attack and charged with abandonment of children, endangering the welfare of children, and reckless endangerment.

Despite the extensive publicity campaigns and new programs designed to combat child abuse and neglect, stories like this are still too common. These children are our future; they belong to all of us. No one can afford to sit back and believe that everything is already taken care of. As you read these words, somewhere in America children are being hurt. Their tears will not stop until our society is transformed into one in which all young people can grow up free of the fear of having pain inflicted on their bodies and minds. These children are in serious trouble. They deserve everyone's help.

SOURCES

C H A P T E R 1

1. Information on the Lisa Steinberg case was found in the following sources:

    Life, January 1989, 121; *McCall's,* June 1988, 57; *Newsweek,* 12 December 1988, 61; *People Weekly,* 13 February 1989, 83; *People Weekly,* 23 November 1987, 44; *U.S. News & World Report,* 14 November 1988, 14; *New York Post,* 25 March 1989, 3.

2. *Ladies' Home Journal,* April 1988, 187.

3. Ibid., p. 158.

4. *The Sunday Star-Ledger* newspaper (Newark, New Jersey), 18 February 1989, 51.

C H A P T E R 2

1. *McCall's,* June 1988, 57.

2. *Redbook,* January 1988, 144.

3. *Ladies' Home Journal,* April 1988, 157.

4. *McCall's,* op. cit., 60.

5. *Newsweek,* 12 December 1988, 56.

6. *People Weekly,* 13 February 1989, 121.

7. *Newsweek,* op. cit., 58.

8. *Ladies' Home Journal,* op. cit., 58.

9. *Life,* January 1989, 121.

10. *Newsweek,* op. cit., 59.

11. *McCall's,* op. cit., 59.

12. *Psychology Today,* August 1987, 9.

13. *Ladies' Home Journal,* op. cit., 159.

14. Ibid.

SOURCES

C H A P T E R 3

1–5. Information for source notes 1 through 5 was found in *Newsweek*, 3 October 1988, 48–50.

6–16. Information for source notes 6 through 16 was found in *Redbook*, January 1988, 109–110, 141.

C H A P T E R 4

1. *Time*, 19 October 1987, 68.
2. *The New York Times Magazine*, 14 September 1986, 58–62.
3. *Time*, op cit.
4–7. Information for source notes 4 through 7 was found in Crewdson, John, *By Silence Betrayed* (Boston: Little Brown, 1988), 83.
8. *The New York Times*, op. cit.
9. Tower, Cynthia Crosson. *Secret Scars: A Guide for Survivors of Child Sexual Abuse.* (New York: Viking, 1988), 83.
10. Crewdson, op cit.
11. Crewdson, op. cit.
12. *Time*, op. cit.

C H A P T E R 5

1. *People Weekly*, 23 January 1989, 84.
2. Ibid.
3–14. Information for source notes 3 through 14 was found in *U.S. News & World Report*, 13 June 1988, 22, 23, 25, 33, 35.

SOURCES

C H A P T E R   6

1–6. Information for source notes 1 through 6 was found in Roy, Maria, *Children in the Cross Fire: Violence in the Home—How Does It Affect Our Children?* (Deerfield Beach, Florida: Health Communications, Inc., 1988), 60, 61, 68.

7. Robert Sadoff, M.D. Transcript #07095 from the "Donohue" show. Multimedia Entertainment, Inc., 1984:9.

8. *Time,* 19 October 1987, 68.

9. *Ladies' Home Journal,* May 1987, 22, 25.

C H A P T E R   7

1. *Ladies' Home Journal,* April 1988, 157.

2. Ibid.

3. *McCall's,* June 1988, 62.

4. *Ladies' Home Journal,* op. cit., 163.

5. *McCall's,* op. cit.

6. *Ladies' Home Journal* op. cit.

7–10. Information for source notes 7 through 10 was found in *Newsweek,* 23 November 1987, 70–71.

11–16. Information for source notes 11 through 16 was found in *Newsweek,* 9 May 1988, 74–75.

17. *Newsweek,* 23 November 1987, 70–71.

18. Ibid.

FURTHER
READING

BOOKS

Aho, Jennifer and John W. Petras. *Learning About Sexual Abuse*. Hillside, NJ: Enslow Publishers, 1985.

Crewdson, John. *By Silence Betrayed: The Sexual Abuse of Children in America*. Boston: Little, Brown, 1988.

Franklin, Alfred W., ed. *The Challenge of Child Abuse*. New York: Grune and Stratton, 1978.

Hanson, Ranae. *Institutional Abuse of Children and Youth*. New York: Haworth Press, 1982.

Holm, Marilyn F. *Shall the Circle Be Unbroken? Helping the Emotionally Maltreated Child*. Longmont, CO: Bookmakers Guild, 1986.

Hyde, Margaret O. *Cry Softly! The Story of Child Abuse*. Revised enlarged ed. Louisville, KY: Westminister, 1987.

Kempe, C. Henry and Ray E. Helfer. *The Battered Child*. Revised enlarged ed. Chicago: University of Chicago Press, 1982.

Koons, Carolyn. *Beyond Betrayal*. New York: Harper & Row, 1987.

Mrazek, Patricia and C. H. Kempe. *Sexually Abused Children and Their Families*. Elmsford, NY: Pergamon, 1981.

Newberger, Eli H. *Child Abuse*. Boston: Little, Brown, 1982.

Polansky, Norman A. *Damaged Parents: An Anatomy of Child Neglect.* Chicago: University of Chicago Press, 1981.

Rush, Florence. *The Best-Kept Secret: Sexual Abuse of Children.* Englewood Cliffs, NJ: Prentice Hall, 1980.

Sloan, Irving J. *Child Abuse: Governing Laws and Legislation.* Dobbs Ferry, NY: Oceana, 1981.

Thompson, Barbara C. *Child Abuse.* Independence, MO: Herald House, 1981.

Volpe, David. *Maltreatment of the School-aged Child.* Lexington, MA: Lexington Books, 1980.

ARTICLES

"Abuse in the Name of Protecting Children" (problems with the child protection system), by Robert L. Emans, *Education Digest,* November 1987, 36.

"Abused Child, Troubled Adult: A Life of Trauma Awaits Young Victims," by Lynne S. Dulmas, *Health,* May 1988, 18.

"Abused Children Learn to Play Again" (nursery schools for needy children), by Judith Newman, *Ms.,* December 1986, 24.

"The Death of Dayna: Behind the Curtains, Scenes of Dickensian Horror," by Frank Trippett, *Time,* 31 October 1988, 19.

"The Divided Self (multiple personality linked to child abuse), by Paul Chance, *Psychology Today,* September 1986, 72.

"Hidden Histories on Death Row" (juveniles sentenced to death found to have history of brain damage, psychiatric disorders, and abuse), *Science News*, 31 October 1987, 287.

"How to Keep Your Kids Safe" (investigating child care and signs of sexual abuse; special report on child sexual abuse), by Marianna Jacobbi and Rosalind Wright, *McCall's*, February 1987, 95.

"Incest Survivors Who Sue," by Anthony Astrachan and Bonnie Freer, *Glamour*, June 1988, 74.

"Mission" (woman makes financial sacrifices to aid in abuse prevention), *Life*, July 1988, 13.

"Ombudsman of Child Abuse" (Dr. Frederick C. Green of the National Committee for Prevention of Child Abuse), *Ebony*, February 1987, 82.

"Our Daughter Was Sexually Abused" (includes related articles: if your child is a victim, signs of possible abuse, the decision to go to court, resources), by Shirley Leonard, *Parents Magazine*, November 1988, 158.

"Somebody Else's Kids: On the Streets with Our Teenage Runaways, Where the Dead End Is Deadlier than Ever," by Pete Axthelm, *Newsweek*, 25 April 1988, 64.

"When She Was Bad: A Battered Child Grows Up," by Anna Wells, *Mademoiselle*, November 1986, 210.

ORGANIZATIONS
THAT CAN HELP

The following organizations are involved in the fight to prevent child abuse:

CHILD ABUSE LISTENING MEDIATION
P.O. Box 718   (805) 682-1366
Santa Barbara, California 93102
Social service program to prevent and treat child sexual abuse, physical abuse, and emotional abuse. Offers early intervention for stressed families.

CHILD WELFARE LEAGUE OF AMERICA
440 First Street NW   (202) 638-2952
Washington, DC 20001
Addresses the improvement of care and services for deprived, dependent, or neglected children, youth, and their families.

CHILDREN'S RIGHTS OF AMERICA
12551 Indian Rocks Rd., Suite 11   (813) 593-0090
Largo, Florida 33544
Provides services to families of missing and exploited children.

CLEARINGHOUSE ON CHILD ABUSE
AND NEGLECT INFORMATION
P.O. Box 1182   (703) 821-2086
Washington, DC 20013
Government agency disseminating information and materials on child abuse and neglect.

DEFENSE FOR CHILDREN INTERNATIONAL – UNITED STATES OF AMERICA

210 Forsyth Street   (212) 353-0951
New York, New York 10002

Seeks to promote and protect the rights of children as defined by national and international legislation.

FIND THE CHILDREN

11811 West Olympic Boulevard   (213) 477-6721
Los Angeles, California 90064

Acts as an information clearinghouse for groups actively searching for missing children.

INSTITUTE FOR THE COMMUNITY AS EXTENDED FAMILY

P.O. Box 952   (408) 280-5055
San Jose, California 95108

Aids in the prevention and treatment of child abuse through training and self-help groups.

INTERNATIONAL INSTITUTE OF CHILDREN'S NATURE AND THEIR RIGHTS

3801 Connecticut Avenue NW
Suite 314   (202) 364-8203
Washington, DC 20008

Conducts medical, social, and legal research on children, devoting special attention to the treatment of children in the court processes and to the medical and legal rights of children.

INTERNATIONAL SOCIETY FOR THE PREVEN-
TION OF CHILD ABUSE AND NEGLECT
1205 Oneida Street   (303) 321-3963
Denver, Colorado 80220
    Provides a forum for sharing knowledge and experience
with the aim of alleviating child abuse and neglect.

NATIONAL CENTER FOR MISSING AND
EXPLOITED CHILDREN
1835 K Street NW, Suite 700   (202) 634-9821
Washington, DC 20006
    Aids parents and law enforcement agencies in prevent-
ing child exploitation and in locating missing children.

NATIONAL CENTER FOR THE PROSECUTION
OF CHILD ABUSE
1033 N. Fairfax Street, Suite 200   (703) 739-0321
Alexandria, Virginia 22314
    Serves as an advocate for victims of child abuse and pro-
motes the prosecution and conviction of child abusers.

NATIONAL COMMITTEE FOR THE PREVENTION
OF CHILD ABUSE
3325 S. Michigan Avenue, Suite 950   (312) 663-3520
Chicago, Illinois 60604
    Serves as an advocate organization to prevent the neglect
and physical, emotional, and sexual abuse of children.

ODYSSEY INSTITUTE CORPORATION
817 Fairfield Avenue   (203) 334-3488
Bridgeport, Connecticut 06604
Provides research, education, and child advocacy programs on issues of serious concern to children.

PARENTS AGAINST MOLESTERS
P.O. Box 3557   (804) 465-1582
Portsmouth, Virginia 23701
Promotes awareness and prevention of child molestation.

PARENTS ANONYMOUS
6733 S. Sepulveda Boulevard, Suite 270   (213) 410-9732
Los Angeles, California 90045
(1,500 groups nationwide)
Aims to rehabilitate child abusers and to ensure the physical and emotional well-being of their children.

INDEX

ABOUT THE
AUTHOR

ELAINE LANDAU has a bachelor's degree in English and journalism from New York University and a master's degree in library and information science from Pratt Institute.

Having worked as a newspaper reporter and editor, she is presently the director of the Sparta Public Library in Sparta, New Jersey. Elaine Landau has written over twenty books and articles for young people on contemporary subjects.

DATE DUE